# On Christian Belief

*On Christian Belief* offers a defence of realism in the philosophy of religion. It argues that religious belief – with particular reference to Christian belief – is not something unlike any other kind of belief, but is cognitive, making claims about what is real, and is open to rational discussion between believers and non-believers.

The author begins by providing a critique of several views which try either to describe a faith without cognitive context, or to justify believing on non-cognitive grounds. He then discusses what sense can be made of the phenomenon of religious conversion by realists and non-realists. After a chapter on knowledge in general, he defends the idea that religious knowledge is very like other knowledge, in being based on reliable testimony, sifted by reason and tested by experience. The logical status of the content of religious belief is then discussed, with reference to Christianity.

**Andrew Collier** is Professor of Philosophy at the University of Southampton and has previously lectured at Warwick, Sussex and Bangor universities. His recent publications include *Being and Worth*, which extends realism to ethics, and *Christianity and Marxism*, which aims to reconcile these two world views.

**Routledge studies in critical realism**
Edited by Margaret Archer, Roy Bhaskar,
Andrew Collier, Tony Lawson and Alan Norrie

Critical realism is one of the most influential new developments in the philosophy of science and in the social sciences, providing a powerful alternative to positivism and post-modernism. This series will explore the critical realist position in philosophy and across the social sciences.

*Also published by Routledge:*
## CRITICAL REALISM: INTERVENTIONS
Edited by Margaret Archer, Roy Bhaskar,
Andrew Collier, Tony Lawson and Alan Norrie

**Critical Realism**
Essential readings
*Edited by Margaret Archer, Roy Bhaskar, Andrew Collier, Tony Lawson and Alan Norrie*

**The Possibility of Naturalism,** third edition
A Philosophical critique of the contemporary human sciences
*Roy Bhaskar*

**Being and Worth**
*Andrew Collier*

**Quantum Theory and the Flight from Realism**
Philosophical responses to quantum mechanics
*Christopher Norris*

**From East to West**
Odyssey of a soul
*Roy Bhaskar*

**Realism and Racism**
Concepts of race in sociological research
*Bob Carter*

**Rational Choice Theory**
Resisting colonisation
*Edited by Margaret Archer and Jonathan Q Tritter*

**Explaining Society**
Critical realism in the social sciences
*Berth Danermark, Mats Ekström, Jan Ch Karlsson and Liselotte Jakobsen*

**Critical Realism and Marxism**
*Edited by Andrew Brown, Steve Fleetwood and John Michael Roberts*

**Critical Realism in Economics**
*Edited by Steve Fleetwood*

**Realist Perspectives on Management and Organisations**
*Edited by Stephen Ackroyd and Steve Fleetwood*

**After International Relations**
Critical realism and the (re)construction of world politics
*Heikki Patomaki*

# On Christian Belief

A defence of a cognitive conception of religious belief in a Christian context

**Andrew Collier**

Routledge
Taylor & Francis Group

LONDON AND NEW YORK

First published 2003
by Routledge
11 New Fetter Lane, London EC4P 4EE

Simultaneously published in the USA and Canada
by Routledge
29 West 35th Street, New York, NY 10001

*Routledge is an imprint of the Taylor & Francis Group*

© 2003 Andrew Collier

Typeset in Times by
Rosemount Typing Services, Thornhill, Dumfriesshire

Printed and bound in Great Britain by
MPG Books Ltd, Bodmin

*British Library Cataloguing in Publication Data*
A catalogue record for this book is available from the British Library

*Library of Congress Cataloging in Publication Data*
Collier, Andrew, 1944–
    On Christian belief : a defence of a cognitive conception of religious
    belief in a Christian context / Andrew Collier.
        p. cm.
    Includes bibliographical references (p. ) and index.
    1. Philosophy and religion. 2. Faith and reason. I. Title.

BR100.C73 2003
231'.042–dc21

                                                    2002037156

ISBN 0–415–31522–0

# Contents

# Foreword

The aim of this foreword is to prevent certain misunderstandings, first of all (briefly) about the theme of the book as stated in the title, and secondly (at some length) about several fundamental concepts with which I am concerned.

This is a book of philosophy, not of theology. I do not aim principally to defend the truth or rationality of any particular Christian belief. I aim to show that the sort of belief involved in Christianity is cognitive in nature, can be rational, and is made rational by things very like those which make other sorts of belief rational. It might be thought that for this reason the title 'on religious belief' would have been better. However, although some of my arguments could be used to defend the rationality of those other religions which claim to base themselves on God's self-revelation through scriptures – namely Judaism, Islam and the Bahai faith – there are so many arguments in the book that apply only to Christianity that it would be arrogant to claim to speak for religion in general.

In defending the rationality of Christian belief, I am defending its claim to constitute knowledge. Since it has become almost a received opinion that Christian belief is 'faith' and that faith is not the same thing as knowledge, I want to get clear some points about the various meanings of words like 'faith', 'belief' and 'knowledge', and their mutual relations. I shall be pointing out different uses of the words, but I shall also be stating how I use the words and why.

## Belief

(1) I take it that the primary and central meaning of the verb 'believe' is 'regard as true'. If we say 'John believes that there is life on Mars', we would expect John to answer 'yes' to the question 'is there life on Mars?'.

That is the explicit content of the belief. But I think that there is an implicit content too. In expressing the belief that there is life on Mars – i.e. in claiming that there is life on Mars – John is tacitly claiming that there are good grounds why he believes that. If someone were to say 'why do you believe that?' and John replied 'no reason – it's just a guess', they would be justified in replying 'you don't really believe it then'. A guess, or a liking to imagine that something is true, is not a belief. One may well have beliefs that one cannot spell out the grounds for. I may not be able to say how I came to believe that Glasgow is the largest city in Scotland, but I could give grounds: I could say 'I must have read it in reliable sources, and I have never heard it called into question', or simply 'everybody says so, and I don't see why they should be lying or misinformed'. Most of our beliefs are probably like this. What would not make sense would be to claim to believe something (in this sense of holding it for true) without ever having been given reason to think the belief true. Such 'belief' would have to be redescribed as 'pretending to believe' or 'imagining' or 'entertaining the idea'.

One more point needs to be made about belief in this sense. I would not say that I believe something unless I understand what it would be for it to be true. I cannot believe a statement whose meaning I don't understand. Yet I may well believe that a statement that I don't understand expresses something true. For instance, there are many statements in the sciences that I don't understand, but I know that those who do understand them and are in a position to judge their truth hold that they are true, and I accept this on their authority. I make this distinction because I don't think that a belief that a certain sentence expresses something (I know not what) that is true can have any significance in religion. Religious beliefs are meant to affect people's lives, and only beliefs in the sense which implies understanding what is believed can do that. Of course, there is another sense in which one may very well not understand 'what is believed', namely one may not understand how the fact that is believed came about. I do not understand how they could make a bridge with a span of 1,410 metres, or how they discovered quarks, or how a Christian can vote Tory, but there is no problem about believing these things. The difficulty in understanding *how* something happened is no obstacle to believing *that* it happened. But one cannot believe that something happened without understanding *what* (supposedly) happened. So there is no objection to the many Christian hymns which express lack of understanding of what God has done (Charles Wesley's 'And can it be', for instance). But when people say things like 'I can't understand what it means for God to be three persons but one God, yet I believe it', there *is* a problem. They can only mean 'I believe that the sentence "God is three persons but one God" expresses something true'. And that statement can have no significance for the faith of the utterer.

(2) The term 'belief' is also sometimes used for opinions about morality, as for instance 'I believe that cruelty is always wrong' or 'I believe that truthfulness is a more important virtue than prudence'. This usage conceals a variety of views about how moral beliefs are related to other beliefs and in what sense if at all they can be true. There are the views (A) that moral beliefs follow from cognitive beliefs and can therefore be true or false; for instance, it might be claimed that from the straightforward fact that statement S is not true, it follows that it would normally be wrong to make people believe that S is true. Hence, 'it is wrong to make people believe that S' would be true because it follows from the true statement that S is false; (B) that moral beliefs don't follow cognitive beliefs but can nevertheless be true or false to some specifically moral facts; for instance, someone might hold that the statement 'murder is wrong' is true, though there are no 'brute' (that is, non-moral) facts which make it true; (C) that moral beliefs can't be true or false, since they are matters of opinion, not of fact. I hold (A), but I shall treat the term 'moral belief' as neutral between these three theories (even though some who hold (C) would prefer, not unreasonably, to use another word than 'belief').

(3) As has often been noted, there is in English a peculiar use of the verb to believe which occurs only in the first person. There are similar usages in other languages. This use is not to indicate a knowledge claim (the standard use of the verb to believe), but to disavow knowledge and instead proffer a tentative opinion. Thus, if you ask John 'is there life on Mars?' and he says 'I believe so', he is probably not expressing the belief that there is life on Mars, but rather showing that he has no such belief, only a tentative opinion. So that, paradoxical as it may sound, to report 'John believes that there is life on Mars' would be false, if he had only said 'I believe so' rather than 'yes'. An accurate report of his opinion would be more like 'John thinks it likely that there is life on Mars'.

I do not think that this usage has any particular importance for our understanding of knowledge and belief. It does not imply that there is any subjective or psychological difference between cases of knowledge and other cases of belief (see below).

Sometimes the word 'belief' is used as a synonym for 'faith' in any of the senses listed below. I shall not use it in these senses.

## Knowledge

I am referring here to the sort of knowledge that can be expressed in propositions, that is, statements of what is the case. I am not assuming that all knowledge can; there is knowledge by acquaintance – the sense in which one knows a person or place – and practical knowledge or knowhow, as well as knowledge by description, and these both have their place in religious knowledge too. Furthermore, much propositional knowledge is not *merely* propositional but also experiential, and this goes for all genuine religious knowledge. But, for reasons which will become clear in the next two chapters, propositional knowledge has an essential role. I take it that whatever else knowledge is, it is at least true belief. So each case of knowledge is a case of belief. Also, I think it follows from my account of belief in sense (1) that every case of belief is thought by the believer to be a case of knowledge. Knowing something does not feel any different from just believing it. To be a case of knowledge, a belief must be true, but also its truth must be no accident. Modern scientists know that matter is composed of atoms, but Democritus did not know it, though he truly believed it. Much ink could be (and has been) spilt spelling out exactly what this 'no accident' clause means. All I need to state here is that in the case of knowledge the truth of the belief in some way explains the occurrence of the belief, and hence that the occurrence of the belief constitutes evidence for its truth.

Perhaps this is the place to get out of the way one bugbear which has haunted philosophy for a long time, particularly since Descartes: the idea of certainty or indubitability as a defining feature of knowledge. If some sort of objective certainty – logical indubitability – is concerned, this is not to be had. All truth claims, precisely because they are claims about how things stand in the objective world, independently of the making of the claims, are fallible, and logically open to challenge and possible refutation. And if on the other hand a subjective feeling of certainty is meant, this is simply of no account. One may feel certain for all sorts of reasons. One may even feel certain that something is so while being rationally convinced that it is most unlikely. So nothing I say about belief, knowledge or faith will imply anything about any feeling of certainty, or any logical indubitability.

## Faith

It would be useful to draw a sharp distinction between belief and faith, though not all languages make this distinction, and it is not always made in English either. Sometimes 'faith' is simply used as a synonym for 'belief' in sense (1). But I think we need to distinguish three other senses.

(1) Faith is sometimes used to mean belief the grounds for which are authority rather than experience or deduction. Belief on grounds of authority need not be irrational – it includes all of lay people's belief about scientific matters, for example. Where true and rational, belief on the grounds of authority may constitute knowledge. I know (on authority) that water = $H_2O$ for example. Hence the old distinction between faith in this sense and knowledge is a mistaken one. Indeed, as we shall see, most of our knowledge is, and all of it presupposes, faith in this sense. There is nothing particularly religious about it – it includes all our knowledge of the past, lay people's knowledge of science, and much else. I shall not use 'faith' in this sense when speaking in my own person, since it evokes the mistaken contrast between belief grounded in authority, and knowledge.

(2) 'Faith' is sometimes used to mean belief without grounds. In popular usage, this use has nearly supplanted all the others, to the extent that, were the word 'faith' not so embedded in the Christian tradition, it might be better to drop the word and find another. For there is no place for faith in this sense in religious life. Anyone who said 'there is life on Mars, but there is no reason whatever to think so' would not be taken seriously, and rightly so. As C.S. Lewis says somewhere, if you make up a piece of nonsense, it does not become sense just because you say it about God. To believe while believing that there are no grounds for the belief is contradictory; to act as if one did so is to base one's life on make-believe. It is faith only in the sense of Sartre's 'bad faith'. I fear most readers will regard these last remarks as paradoxical; I hope to justify them in the course of the book.

(3) The sense of 'faith' in which this concept is central to the Christian tradition is *trust*. This is what Luther meant by faith, and mis-understanding of this has led to the saddest distortion of Protestantism – the idea that holding some doctrine to be true is itself meritorious (as if that could be, as Luther expressly denies, an act of will). The New

Testament itself seems to use 'faith' to mean trust: to have faith in God is to trust him. The New Testament translation called the *The Jewish New Testament* actually uses the word 'trust' instead of 'faith'. But faith in this sense is not unrelated to belief in the first sense (cognitive belief). I think the logical and causal relations between the two things are as follows:

non-identity. Faith as trust is not itself a belief but an emotion;
presupposition. All emotions presuppose beliefs. Trust presupposes the belief that the trusted person exists, and is benevolent and reliable;
rational support. Given certain beliefs about a person (which will include the beliefs supporting the conclusion that they are benevolent and reliable) it will be rational to trust that person, and irrational not to.

Trust can also be part of the grounds for believing something; if you trust someone, you will normally believe what they say. This is the connection between trust and faith in the first sense, that is believing on the authority of someone's testimony. But trust cannot be the ground for those beliefs which it presupposes itself. You cannot justify the belief in someone's trustworthiness by the emotion of trusting them, only the other way round.

Of course, it may happen that trust can lead causally to belief in someone's trustworthiness. One way in which this can happen involves irrationality: one may feel strongly inclined to trust someone, and so come to believe that they are trustworthy through wishful thinking. On this phenomenon rests every successful seduction or confidence trick. But the following scenario can also occur: someone is offered help that they badly need by a stranger, whom they have no solid grounds for believing trustworthy. If they accept the help and the stranger is ill-intentioned, they put themselves in danger. They take a chance and trust the stranger, who turns out to be trustworthy, and all is well. It is because they have taken the chance that they afterwards came to the well-founded belief that the stranger was trustworthy. The significance of this example is that some people have claimed that religious faith is like that. This is, for me at least, the only attractive version of non-cognitivism in the philosophy of religion.

But I suspect that the plausibility of this example flows from its being underdescribed. In such a case the person who trusts the stranger may do so on the basis of subtle signs of trustworthiness that the stranger has given, which may be good grounds for believing in it, even though one may be unable to spell out what they are. If this is *not* the case, however, and trust has to be given completely blind, I suspect that what is given is actually something less than trust. Rather, one acts 'as if' one trusts the stranger, yet does not escape the nagging doubt 'what if he turns out to be a scoundrel?'. In either of these cases, the account of trust-leading-to-the-belief-which-justifies-it breaks down, as does the plausibility of the parallel with religious belief.

These definitions set out the destination of this book. Christian faith (trust) is rational if it is founded on certain beliefs about God. Those beliefs are straightforward cognitive beliefs – truth claims – and they are rational if we have good cognitive grounds for them, just as in any other area of knowledge.

Before I leave this terminological section, a few words are needed about the technical terms that I am using. I am actually defending three related theses about Christian belief: that it is *cognitive*, that it is (or can be) *rational*, and that it is to be interpreted in a *realist* sense. By 'cognitive' I mean that it is a belief in the sense of a claim to knowledge, not of an attitude or disposition. Cognitive matters are knowledge, belief, evidence, logical relations between beliefs. They traditionally contrast with emotive matters and matters relating to action. This is only an analytical contrast, that is to say, all beliefs evoke feelings and all emotions involve beliefs, all beliefs can affect action and all actions involve beliefs. There are nöt three 'faculties' in the mind, reason, emotion and will, there are only emotions, that is, beliefs charged with feeling. But one can abstract out the cognitive element and distinguish cognitive relations (for example, logical relations of belief to belief, epistemic relations of belief to evidence). The term 'cognitive' has nothing to do with computer models of the mind.

Beliefs can be *rational* (based on considerations relevant to their truth) or *irrational* (based on considerations irrelevant to their truth). Of course, emotions and actions can be rational or irrational as well, but since rationality has to do with relating to things as they really are in themselves, the rationality of emotions or acts is always a function of the rationality of the beliefs that they involve. (See my book *Being and Worth* for an account of rationality.) In this book I am not just claiming that

Christian beliefs are cognitive, but asking under what conditions they can be rational.

Thirdly, if Christian beliefs are cognitive – are claims to knowledge – they must be interpreted in a realist sense; that is to say, in saying the Creed I am expressing beliefs but I am not talking about my beliefs or any other attitudes of mine. I am talking about God. I intend to say what is objectively true. This means that anyone who says the opposite is contradicting me, and we can't both be right. If I say 'I like spicy food' and you say 'I don't like spicy food', we have not contradicted each other, and there is no question of either of us being right or wrong; if I say 'there is a squirrel up that tree' and you say 'there isn't a squirrel up that tree', then we have contradicted each other and we can't both be right. Saying 'God exists' is more like saying 'there is a squirrel up that tree' than like saying 'I like spicy food'. Of course, there are differences between saying 'God exists' and saying 'there is a squirrel up that tree', but they stem from the nature of God and of squirrels, not from any difference in the use of language or the kind of knowledge. One doesn't in the usual run of things find God by looking up a tree. But the theist and the atheist can no more both be right than the squirrelist and the asquirrelist. To most Christians, this will seem too obvious to need saying. It will never have occurred to them that their faith could be interpreted in other than a realist way – why should it? But non-realism is quite common among theologians and philosophers of religion. The distinction between the realist, who in saying 'God exists' means to assert that there is a Being who pre-existed and is independent of all human minds and material things, and the non-realist, for whom 'God exists' is only a statement about their own attitude or the place of humankind in nature, is much more radical than other divisions within Christianity – divisions between Catholic, Protestant and Orthodox, or between evangelical and liberal Protestants, for instance.

Finally, there is one more pair of words my use of which I want to make clear. These are the adjective 'objective' and the noun 'objectivity'. I use 'objective' to mean independent of a subject: objective knowledge is knowledge which is true independently of any knower; objective values are values whose value is independent of any valuer. The objectivity of a fact is its holding independently of any awareness or description of it. Objectivity as a human virtue is the quality of letting one's beliefs be determined by the way things are rather than by anything contributed by us. It is necessary to say this for two reasons.

(1) It has become fashionable in certain circles to play on the etymology and ancient use of the word 'object' and its derivatives, and claim that objectivity is by definition correlative of subjectivity, and hence that objectivity in the sense just defined is impossible. This is a mere verbal trick: objectivity may once have meant being an object for a subject, but now it means just the opposite.

(2) There is a tendency in existentialist philosophy to use 'objective' in a sense which perhaps includes the sense which I give, but which also includes connotations of '*Entzauberung*', value-neutrality, quantifiability, impoverishment relative to the rich world of lived experience, inability to speak to the heart. (There is a corresponding existentialist use of 'subjectivity', which has none of the connotations of subjectivist theories of knowledge or ethics.) None of these connotations attach to objectivity in the sense I give it. God, values and qualitative distinctions are all objective on my account.

Now, at the end of this foreword, there is something that needs to be said. I wrote the foreword to avoid misunderstanding by making it clear what I took certain words to mean, or at least what I mean by them and regard as their most useful uses. Yet it occurs to me that if I have succeeded in getting the reader to use the words as I do – to use 'faith' to mean trust in God, founded on belief that he exists and is good, to use 'belief' to mean a claim that a statement is true and has evidence to show that it is true, to accept that there can be religious 'knowledge' then I have already done what I set out to do in this book as a whole. And yet all the arguments are still to come. (I follow Judaeo-Christian tradition in using the pronoun 'he' to refer to God. 'She' would be equally theologically acceptable since God is not sexed and made both men and women in his image, but one has to choose. 'It' or 'he or she' would not be acceptable.) If you are not convinced by my arguments as I set them out, you will doubtless continue to use the words 'faith', 'belief' and 'knowledge' in ways different from mine. I only ask that you follow my arguments carefully and consider them seriously.

# Introduction

The foregoing account of belief, including religious belief, is a cognitive one: to say 'I believe in God' is (among other things) to claim to know that God exists; it is not to express an emotion or a practical resolve, though if the belief is sincerely held it will give rise to emotions and practical resolves. This account of religious belief, and the corresponding account of divine revelation as communicating knowledge of God that we would not have had without it, is deeply unfashionable among Protestant philosophers of religion, and many Protestant theologians. Religious beliefs are said to be more akin to moral beliefs, in the sense that 'people ought to be kind to animals' is a moral belief. Behind this, in turn, is a long-standing philosophical position (a false one, in my opinion) about the nature of moral beliefs and moral psychology. Moral beliefs are treated as free-floating imperatives, not grounded in any statements of fact, and correspondingly statements of fact are denied to be reasons for action. This is often presented as a logical point: you can't derive imperatives from indicatives – though why anyone should obey an imperative without some indicative grounding I can't imagine. The logical point has been sufficiently refuted by Roy Bhaskar's account of explanatory critiques.[1] The underlying error in moral psychology can take two forms: either (with Hume) emotions can be separated from (cognitive) beliefs and said to be the springs of action; or a faculty called *the will*, distinct from both emotion and belief, is postulated, and ascribed the power to make choices ungrounded in beliefs or emotions. As against these views, I am assuming a Spinozist account of action: emotions are the springs of action, and nothing can drive out an emotion but another emotion; so far Hume is right. But emotions involve beliefs: to love someone is to believe that they are in some way good, to fear something is to believe that it is in some way dangerous, and so on. Apparent counter-examples such as irrational phobias and obsessive loves can be explained psychoanalytically in terms of unconscious beliefs. So the way to replace wrong actions by right actions is by replacing irrational emotions by rational ones, and the way to do that is to replace false beliefs by true ones.[2] If religious beliefs are to make us better people, they must do so by virtue of their truth. At this point, however, I part company from Spinoza, who held that true beliefs about God (or *Deus sive Natura*) are deducible geometrically from evident premises. I hold that they can only be based on God's historical self-revelation to us.

I shall shortly look at some non-cognitive accounts of revelation. First though I need to distinguish the contrast between cognitive and non-cognitive revelation from two other contrasts.

(1) We may distinguish two approaches to the Bible as the means of God's revelation: one view (a rather extreme form of fundamentalism) is that God's revelation just consists in the totality of propositions of which the Bible is composed. Probably even the most dyed-in-the-wool fundamentalist does not really believe that the proposition that 'Aram begat Aminadab' is of the same significance as John 3.16. But fundamentalists do sometimes say that books like Joshua and Judges are just as much God's word as Luke and John, and that there is therefore just as much to learn from them.

Against this, there is the view that 'God's word' in the deepest sense is not the Bible but Christ himself – that only by our knowing Christ can God the Father be revealed to us – and that the Bible is only God's word to the extent that it witnesses to Christ. I take this to be Luther's view, in his Preface to the New Testament, and it is also my own. Now this view is sometimes called a non-propositional view of revelation, because God is revealed not by propositions about him, but by the life and death of Christ. This usage is fair enough, provided that three points are recognised: (i) that a great deal of the revelation in Christ takes place through propositions uttered by Christ; (ii) that much of the revelation in Christ that does not consist in his words can nevertheless be expressed in propositions, and is so within the New Testament, e.g. that God is love, that God does not will that any should perish, and so on; (iii) that we today can only know of Christ from the Bible what has been expressed in propositions, and that any further knowledge of Christ that we may have from personal experience depends upon this propositional knowledge. Hence, the rejection of the idea of revelation as the series of propositions contained in the Bible does not commit us to a non-cognitive notion of revelation, nor to understanding revealed knowledge as inherently non-propositional in nature.

(2) Recent tendencies in theology have foregrounded narrative rather than theoretical theology as the basic form of religious discourse. Certainly those religions which claim to be revealed religions – Judaism, Christianity, Islam, the Bahai faith – start from a narrative, and their revelation is not a matter of timeless truths that anyone might have discovered, but of historically specific events in which God is said to have revealed himself. But several points need to be made about this distinction between narrative theology and theoretical theology. Firstly, knowledge of a narrative is not non-cognitive; narratives are even the paradigm case of objects of cognition. Less disputably than any other form of discourse, a narrative consists of propositions which can be true or false; they communicate information, and only thereby do they prescribe actions or commend values or arouse emotions or establish identities, when they do. So a non-cognitive narrative theology is clearly a non-starter.

Now it may be said: but there are fictional narratives. Indeed there are, and it is characteristic of them that they (unlike, for example, a diatribe composed entirely of imperatives) are constructed *as if* they were true, and their emotive or prescriptive force can only be understood in terms of how we would respond to them if they were true. A sad story recounts fictional events which, if they really happened, would be sad. Some people think there are interesting philosophical problems about the logical status of propositions in fictional contexts. I don't. But there are certainly serious issues about the use of fictional narratives in religion. There is such a use of course: the parables of Jesus make their points as well if they are fictions as they do if they have a historical basis, as Joachim Jeremias suggests some of them have. But it is not a matter of indifference whether Jesus existed, led a good life, proclaimed the coming of the Kingdom of God, died, or was raised from the dead. If it turned out that Jesus didn't exist, or was a double agent in the pay of Herod Antipas, Christians might as well shut up shop. For the point of the gospel narratives is that 'God was in Christ reconciling the world unto himself', and if Jesus did not exist, then he wasn't, and Christians are 'of all men most to be pitied', as Paul says. One can deny this only if one holds that the narratives are *not* essential to Christianity, that they merely serve to illustrate its eternal truths (as some of the parables actually do – hence our indifference to their historical truth).

The truth in narrative theology must be understood in a realist sense: what is special about the gospel narratives is not their narrative form, but their relation to the events that they recount. Narratives are central to Christian theology because the historical events whereby God revealed himself in a particular time and place are central to the life of Christianity. However, the fact that the importance of the narratives rests on something happening in the events recounted which could not have happened were they fictional leads us to the limits of narrative theology. The narrative points beyond itself.

Narrative discourse is not a closed system, unpermeated by theory. The gospel narrative for instance would make no sense without the explanatory ideas that the world is fallen from God its maker and is ruled by the forces of evil, that Jesus was sent by the Father to break their power, and so on. A gospel narrative without this explanatory depth dimension would not only be quite unlike the four Gospels that we have got; it would be a meaningless tale of one thing after another. Apart from which, there are Paul's epistles, which make up much of the New Testament – and the earliest parts of it to be written – and are not narratives at all but depth explanations of the narrative that was at that time transmitted orally, and later recorded in the Gospels.

Now let us consider the supposed contrast between rational and revealed religion. One traditional view is that the theoretical content of religion – theology, if you like – comes in two kinds: natural theology, deduced by pure reason from indubitable premises, and revealed theology, accepted on authority. In the best such accounts (Aquinas's, for instance) reason has a role to play in revealed theology as well; but it is a limited role, the limits being in part external limits on reason rather than internal limits to reason: the dogmas of the Church, for instance, could not be gainsaid. Of course the defender of the rationality of this could argue that there are good reasons for accepting the dogmas of the Church; but if this means agreeing in advance to accept them whatever they are, reason is thereby restricted. In practice no authority would be accepted whatever it said; if the Pope were to declare *ex cathedra* that God had become a little green frog, I am sure Catholics would come to doubt papal infallibility rather than accept this dogma.

From the late Middle Ages on, natural and revealed theology tend to become increasingly polarised. Natural theology gets thinner and thinner in content, and ends in deism; revealed theology takes less and less account of reason. Hume and Kant, the former with his tongue in his cheek, the latter seriously, claim that they have demolished natural theology only to make way for faith – but faith conceived as having no cognitive grounds. It often happens in the history of ideas that a view that was originally held by no one, and invented as a straw man by its opponents, later gains adherents. Hobbes's political philosophy is a refutation of anarchism written at a time when there were no anarchists – then, 150 years later, along came Godwin, and there have been anarchists ever since. Thousands of witches were executed in the early modern period when there were no witches, with the result that there are now an estimated 80,000 witches in England. The frankly irrational faith which Hume set up as an Aunt Sally to shy at has now conquered most of the Protestant world, and is assumed by most unbelievers to be the only meaning that 'faith' ever had.

In order to undo this polarisation, we need to criticise too its medieval starting point, i.e. the division of religious knowledge into that provided by pure reason and that derived from authority. For the Protestant critics of natural theology and the Enlightenment critics of authority were both right about something, but they came together in the wrong way to produce this polarisation – or rather to complete it, for it is already going on in William of Ockham's work. What should have been said, I think, is something like this.

(1) No knowledge, whether sacred or secular, is deduced by pure reason from indubitable premises. Apparent exceptions like mathematics are ultimately tautologous, and so tell us nothing about how the world is. So from a philosophical point of view, we can hardly expect arguments like the ontological and cosmological proofs of the existence of God to work, since that sort of argument doesn't work in any other contexts. And in fact I think that these arguments don't work, for reasons which have often been set out and I don't need to repeat here.[3] Arguments from particular aspects of the world could in principle work. But (a) like other arguments from empirical facts they will be fallible and establish at most likelihoods rather than certainties, and (b) from a Christian point of view they are theologically suspect – an issue to which I shall return.

(2) All our knowledge about the world – secular as well as religious – is based primarily upon authority in the sense that it is based on hearsay, and authority is simply hearsay that one has reasons to believe reliable. But this authority is not above reason; it must be constantly sifted and criticised by reason, and this should apply both to secular knowledge (history, science, news, etc.) and religious (revealed theology). It is no use a fundamentalist saying 'who are you to criticise God?', since what is at stake in criticising putatively revealed knowledge is precisely whether it comes from God or not.

In short, the alternative to the polarisation of reason and revelation is: all religious knowledge is revealed theology, but reason has the same rights here as in any other area of knowledge; that is, it should be completely unfettered. That is my conclusion for the practice of religious thinking. But to get there I have to refute three formidable positions: (i) that what is revealed in revelation and accepted in faith is not knowledge or belief at all, but something non-cognitive ('faith without belief'); (ii) that while religion involves cognitive beliefs, they are to be accepted on non-cognitive grounds ('belief without cognitive grounds'); and (iii) that there can be no rational grounds for accepting revealed beliefs. I shall criticise several variants of the first two positions in chapters 1 to 3; in chapter 4 I shall argue that the phenomenon of religious conversion requires a cognitive account of religious belief for its intelligibility; in chapter 5 I shall outline a general theory of knowledge, and in chapter 6 show how this allows us to see revealed religious knowledge as having grounds much more like those for secular knowledge than is commonly thought. Arguments against the rationality of religious belief are often cast as arguments about the nature of religious language; I shall also discuss problems in this area in chapter 6. I leave these problems until after I have discussed the theory of religious knowledge, since I shall argue that they are not really a separate set of problems, but merely a misleading representation of the problems of the theory of religious knowledge. I shall then make my account more concrete with respect to Christian revelation in chapter 7. The purely revealed character of theology as defended here seems to cut religion off from faith in God as creator, which the cosmological and teleological arguments made central. So I shall also discuss the place of faith in God as creator in chapter 8.

At the risk of repeating myself, a few words need to be said about some features of the last two chapters. I am a philosopher by training, not a theologian, and this book is a work of philosophy, not of theology. Some people might find it surprising that in certain parts of the book there are quite a few quotations from the Bible, and even a certain amount of amateur theology. Let me make it clear in advance why this is.

First of all, let me say that the biblical quotes (taken, incidentally, from various versions of the Bible) are in no way used, as a fundamentalist might use them in a theological argument, as authoritative statements of truth. That would really be unphilosophical, for it would simply raise the question what grounds we have for believing biblical statements to be more reliable than other statements. In a *philosophical* argument, that is the question that the fundamentalist would need to answer. Secondly, there is a certain conception of the relation between philosophy and theology, which was widely held in the Middle Ages, that would make the appearance of biblical texts in a philosophical text look strange. This is the view that philosophy has special premises of its own, based on pure reason, and one part of theology, 'natural theology', is part of philosophy; revealed theology on the other hand takes its premises from the Bible or the dogmas of the Church. I hope I have made it abundantly clear that this is not my conception of philosophy (or theology). In common with most modern philosophers, I hold that philosophy has no special premises or subject matter of its own. What makes it philosophy is the kind of arguments involved. So there should be nothing more surprising about biblical quotations in a work on the philosophy of religion than about descriptions of scientific experiments in a book on the philosophy of science, or references to works of art in a book on aesthetics.

A word is necessary, however, about why I cannot avoid a certain amount of amateur theology in the later part of the book. The question of the possibility of religious knowledge can in large part be answered without reference to the content of religious knowledge. It can be neutral as between different theologies and even different world religions. Most of the first six chapters fall into this category. However, there are other kinds of philosophical question about religious knowledge: firstly, about the sort of thing it is, its logical status: is it in the imperative or the indicative, knowledge of divine commandments or of the divine nature? One cannot answer this without discussing particular candidates for revealed knowledge. This explains the theology in chapter 7. And lastly, the denial of natural theology could be thought to be in contradiction with belief in God as creator, which is part of revealed theology in theistic religions. And it is eminently a function of philosophy to resolve apparent contradictions, whatever discipline they arise from. This goes on in chapter 8.

# 1  Faith without belief I

## Religious feeling

First of all, let me say what I intend to argue. I am in no way trying to play down the role of emotion in religion or in life in general. Emotions are the stuff of human life, and a religion without emotion is a withered up religion. What is at stake is what emotions are. Are they blind feelings, uncriticisable and needing no justification; or do they involve beliefs, which can be true or false? My view is the latter: I am afraid of a Rhodesian Ridgeback since I believe that they are dangerous (one having nearly killed my wife and son). I am angry about the government's pension policy since I believe it is inhumane in its effects. I love God since I believe he first loved us, and showed it in the person of Christ. All these emotions are challengeable and need justification, since all involve beliefs which might be true or false. If someone disagrees with me about pensions, they will provide arguments: that it is possible to live very well on a pension, or that the effect of raising pensions would be some unthinkable disaster, like making well-to-do younger people spend less on cars and mobile phones. If I am not convinced, that is not because my anger is self-justifying, but because I believe the arguments against me are bad ones. If religious emotions are like this, then it is arguments about cognitive beliefs that decide whether they are rational or not. To avoid this cognitivist conclusion, one has to strip emotions of the beliefs that make them the emotions that they are. My argument is against this reduced conception of emotions, and more particularly against views which oscillate between a reduced 'blind feeling' conception of emotion and one which involves beliefs.

The idea of a purely non-cognitive faith has obvious attractions. It relieves the religious person of the duties of epistemic ethics – the duty to ask if one's beliefs are well-founded, if they conflict with other, better-founded beliefs, and so on. If there were no cognitive element in faith, then one really could choose to have faith, without being convinced of anything first. There is also a serious intellectual history to this attraction: from Galileo to Darwin and beyond, there have been a series of seeming clashes between religion and science. In each case, some new scientific discovery has seemed to conflict with some proposition belonging to current religious belief; some believers have dug their heels in and refused to accept the discovery; some have accepted it and lost their faith; some have claimed that what the religious doctrine really meant never conflicted with the science anyway. I take it that the last response has always been the right one, but if it is merely an ad hoc response to each separate discovery, made out of necessity when it becomes clear that the discovery can no longer be rationally denied, then it looks like a retreat, making the best of a bad job, rather than a principled position.

Certainly, in many cases the literalist reading of the Scriptures that generated the science/religion clash has never been universally accepted by believers even before the new discovery, and in some cases looks quite strange even by purely internal criteria. Could anyone who has thought the matter through ever really believe, for instance, that the universe was created in seven literal days, when the sun was not even created till the fourth day (Genesis 1.18)? This was pointed out by the Christian philosopher and martyr Origen, as early as the third century. Nevertheless, it would be much better to solve the religion/science clash once and for all, by showing that they could not clash in principle because they are about different things. And the simplest and most radical way to do this would be by showing that while science is cognitive, religion is not. We could then dismiss in advance any supposed conflict between religion and any cognitive discipline, whether science, history or 'commonsense'. There are of course more moderate ways of marking off religion from science, without abandoning a realist and cognitive account of religious belief. None can be certain of avoiding all conflict, but the area of possible conflict gets quite small, provided the realist is not an extreme fundamentalist who believes in the literal inerrancy of Scripture. Such a fundamentalist will, I think, inevitably confront a few conflicts with science (for example about Joshua making the sun stand still – Joshua 10.13) and indeed with logic (for example trying to reconcile Matthew's and Luke's accounts of the fate of Judas Iscariot – Matthew 27.3–8, Acts 1.18–19). But an account which is realist about God and his acts and hence cognitivist about belief, but which is not fundamentalist in this sense, can usually avoid science/religion clashes, rather as chemistry does not clash with linguistics, though both are cognitive, simply because they are about different things. However, this does not definitively avoid such clashes since two sciences with different subject-matters may overlap (to use Aquinas's example: both the astronomer and the physicist prove that the Earth is round – so much for the legend that the medievals thought it was flat!). Theology and history for instance overlap, so that a historical proof that Jesus never existed would refute Christianity, although a proof that Buddha never existed would not refute Buddhism, since the life of Buddha is not part of the religious subject-matter of Buddhism, while the life of Jesus is part of the religious subject-matter of Christianity. Buddhism does, however, contain some general doctrines which are propositional and have entailments and contradictories, and hence which can be defended as true or criticised as false by rational, if somewhat metaphysical, arguments. The non-cognitive account of religion though, if true, would make 'faith' completely rationally unassailable, come what may in the cognitive disciplines (though by the same token, it would make it rationally undefendable).

I shall now consider four versions of the non-cognitive account of 'faith': two, concerned with religious feeling, in the remainder of this chapter, and two, concerned with 'moral faith', in the next.

## 1   Bare feeling

Many non-cognitivists say that religion is based on feeling. But for this idea to do the work of parrying cognitive arguments, it must take a rather extreme form. It is likely that no one has ever consistently held this extreme form of the view, but some have seemed to slide between it and other, more moderate feeling-oriented accounts of religion. The plausibility of feeling-theology depends on a less extreme form being adopted, but the invulnerability to rational criticism depends on the extreme version. The extreme version is that religion is based on bare feeling, that is to say, feeling without any cognitive content or presuppositions.

Are there bare feelings? Perhaps there are: low-key nausea, for example, of the type that does not presage vomiting, could be said to be entirely non-cognitive; pains, if analytically distinguished from the information about bodily ailments which, to any adult, they convey;

euphoria, induced by a long walk in the country but not *about* the long walk in the country. For of course as soon as a feeling comes to be about something, it is no longer purely non-cognitive: it involves beliefs about what it is about. If you express your euphoria by saying even 'it's good to be alive', a passing Buddhist may tell you 'on the contrary, the first of the Four Noble Truths tells us that all existence is misery', and, if you stick to your guns, you have all the makings of an entirely cognitive religious argument.

So in order to stay non-cognitive, a feeling has to remain pretty thin: much too thin to be identified as religious. Can we fill it out enough to identify it as religious without implicating beliefs which can be assessed as true or false? I think not. Take Schleiermacher's 'feeling of absolute dependence' for instance. One can immediately ask 'but are we absolutely dependent? If so, what on? Is that which we are dependent on worthy of worship?' – and so on. One might hold, like Berdyaev, that the Divinity wills us to be independent – rather as when Ezekiel prostrates himself before a vision of God, he is told 'Son of man, stand up, I am going to speak to you' (Ezekiel 2.1). These issues take us way beyond bare feeling. Indeed, knowing Schleiermacher's love of Spinoza, one might think that the 'feeling of absolute dependence' is none other than the feeling that Spinoza's metaphysics is true; that is a feeling that those of us who have read Spinoza sometimes have. But Spinoza would be the last person to think that such a feeling was evidence that his metaphysics was true.

The objection to Schleiermacher is not that he overstated the importance of emotion – that would be hard to do. It is that he understates the importance of belief in emotional life. In this respect he ought to be *more* Spinozist. Of course, while basing religion on emotion, he wrote a whole book on doctrine, and so can hardly mean to drive a wedge between emotion and belief. But as soon as it is admitted that emotions involve beliefs, it becomes possible to criticise those beliefs and hence those emotions on the basis of other beliefs, that is 'faith' becomes vulnerable to cognitive criticism and requires cognitive defence. The decision between one emotion and another rests on an input of beliefs.

And such is surely our experience with non-religious emotions: I am made sad by the death of my friend, angry by the government's welfare cuts, and so on. Religious emotions are no different: one may hate God because one believes he is a merciless judge or love him because one believes he is a compassionate father or fear him because one believes he is a mighty ruler or feel totally indifferent to him because one believes he wound up the clock of the universe and left it to tick out unaided, or whatever.

So far, I have discussed 'pure feeling' without textual references, to show that it cannot do the job it is meant to do: if it stays as pure feeling, it gives us too little to be called religion, and if it gives us enough, it goes beyond feeling and makes truth claims about the world. However, I have mentioned Schleiermacher, and since he is one of the 'greats' of Protestant theology, and I may be thought to have been using him as a straw man, I shall now discuss one text by him, namely the second (and crucial) speech from his *On Religion: Speeches to its Cultured Despisers*. (If my purpose were to assess Schleiermacher's work as a whole, I would have to discuss *On Christian Doctrine*, too, and the question as to whether the same questions arise about that text is a complex one. But here I am using Schleiermacher only as an examplar of the theology of feeling, so one text that indisputably belongs to such theology is enough.)

I think it is striking that within a few pages of this speech he has passed from talking about pure experience (which I shall claim is religiously empty) to talking about recognisably religious experience (laden with beliefs); yet he is claiming both religious fullness and belieflessness for what he is talking about.

First, he excludes both metaphysics and morals from religion:

> [Religion] does not wish to determine and explain the universe according to its nature as does metaphysics; it does not desire to continue the universe's development and perfect it by the power of freedom and the divine free choice of a human being as does morals. Religion's essence is neither thinking nor acting, but intuition and feeling.
>
> (p. 22)

I think he is using 'intuition' in the Kantian sense: not a mysterious source of knowledge, but sensation, the effect of the outside world upon us.

I entreat you to become familiar with this concept: intuition of the universe.

All intuition proceeds from an influence of the intuited on the one who intuits, from an original and independent action of the former, which is then grasped, apprehended, and conceived by the latter according to one's own nature.

(pp. 24–5)

He is talking about a sense datum, or rather, since it is not some particular thing but the whole universe that is affecting one, The Sense Datum. It does not include belief:

what you thus intuit and perceive is not the nature of things, but their action upon you. What you know or believe about the nature of things lies far beyond the realm of intuition.

. . . to accept everything individual as part of the whole and everything limited as a representation of the infinite is religion. But whatever would go beyond that and penetrate deeper into the nature and substance of the whole is no longer religion, and will, if it still wants to be regarded as such, inevitably sink back into empty mythology.

(p. 25)

Just as sense-datum theorists thought that it was rash to say 'I saw a dog' and wiser to say more modestly 'I saw a canoid patch of colour', so Schleiermacher is calling The Sense Datum 'religious', but any fuller account of the universe experienced 'mythology'. So far, two comments are required.

(i) Only someone highly trained in abstraction can make the distinction between sense data and the 'nature and substance' of what we see and hear. People had been seeing dogs since the earliest human settlements, but no one before Bertrand Russell had ever spotted a canoid patch of colour. Is it not the same with The Sense Datum? Doubtless the whole universe is having effects on me, but if I attend to the experience of it, I am aware only of entities and laws of which I have concepts and about which I have beliefs.

(ii) Schleiermacher appears to be talking not about some special mystical experience distinct from all particular sensations, but about the experienced effect of the whole universe on one; the whole does not presumably affect us in any way distinct from the totality of effects of particulars; The Sense Datum presumably includes the particular sense data. Salient in my intuition of the universe as I write this are the sight of new-leaved trees in the park outside the window, the sound of a bus revving up, and the click clack of women's shoes on the library floor behind me. But if The Sense Datum were just the sum of such things, it would hardly do the job that Schleiermacher gives it. The clue is in the phrase 'to accept everything individual as a part of the whole and everything limited as a representation of the infinite': I may take the springing into leaf of the trees as a symbol of the fecundity of nature as a whole; but to do so is no longer a naïve intuition of the universe, but one which is informed by an acquired notion of symbolism. And concrete religions have definite doctrines about what symbolises what. The apparent neutrality of The Sense Datum between different systems of dogma, ritual and ethics is only apparent. Schleiermacher goes on to contrast in ancient Greek paganism the 'religion' in which

> they intuited the ever-active, ever-living, and serene activity of the world and its spirit, beyond all change and all the apparent evil that only stems from the conflict of finite forms

with their 'empty mythology' in which they kept 'a wondrous chronicle of the descent of these gods'.

But this is not a distinction between a belief-free intuition and beliefs, but between pantheistic and polytheistic beliefs.

Schleiermacher's next step is to say that the intuition of the universe is inseparably connected with a feeling. However, this feeling will not lead to any particular action:

> [religion's] feelings are supposed to possess us, and we should express, maintain, and portray them.
>
> But should you wish to go beyond that dimension with these feelings, should they cause actual actions and incite you to deeds, then you find yourself in an alien realm. If you still hold this to be religion, however rational and praiseworthy your action may appear, you are absorbed in an unholy superstition.

(pp. 29–30)

But surely there are three things which need to be said about feelings here. (i) They come in different kinds; one may intuit the universe with joy like Spinoza or with misery like the Buddha or with nausea like Sartre. (ii) They generally come with beliefs, and which belief determines which feeling. (iii) They generally give rise to action. One is tempted to paraphrase the Epistle of James and say to Schleiermacher 'show me your feelings without your actions, and I will show you my feelings by my actions'.

Schleiermacher's next step is to point out that our intuition of nature includes all sorts of learnt concepts; I couldn't agree more, but he seems unaware that this is a radical departure from beliefless feeling.

> Certainly a greater yield is vouchsafed to us who have been permitted by a richer age to penetrate deeper into nature's interior. Its chemical powers, the eternal laws according to which bodies themselves are formed and destroyed, these are the phenomena in which we intuit the universe most clearly and in a most holy manner.
>
> (p. 36)

This is good Spinozism: we intuit and love not just particular things but the laws of nature. But laws of nature are true – or rather putative laws of nature claim truth and are either true or false. Schleiermacher further says that ideas like individuality and oneness are derived not from nature but from mind (p. 37), and that it is primarily in humanity and in a beloved human individual, rather than in nature, that we find the 'material for religion' (pp. 37–8). Precisely, but here we are no longer talking about The Sense Datum, we are talking about knowledge – knowledge acquired through science and social intercourse and philosophical reflection – and feeling evoked by and attached to it. We are now enjoined to learn from others:

> From these wanderings through the whole realm of humanity, religion then returns to one's own self with sharpened meaning and better formed judgement.
>
> (p. 41)

This feeling seems now to have acquired a practical goal too:

To join the different moments of humanity to one another and, from its succession, to divine the spirit in which the whole is directed, that is religion's highest concern.

(p. 42)

The beliefless, unmotivating intuition of a few pages earlier has been left far behind – and rightly so, for it was an intuition experienced by no one about nothing. But in leaving it behind, he is entering the field of beliefs and practical goals, where he must choose some one religion among others, and contend against the doctrines of others. And indeed he does so:

> there then appears to you the form of an eternal destiny whose features bear completely the mark of this condition, a strange mixture of inflexible obstinacy and deep wisdom, of vulgar, heartless force and heartfelt love of which alternately sometimes the one seizes you and sometimes the other, while each in turn invites you to impotent defiance and childlike resignation. If you then compare the isolated striving of the individual, which has arisen from these contradictory views, with the calm and uniform progress of the whole, you see how the lofty world spirit smilingly strides across all that tumultuously opposes it. You see how the majestic Nemesis unweariedly follows its steps across the earth, how it administers chastisement and punishment to the haughty who resist the god, and how it mows down with an iron hand even the bravest and most excellent who, perhaps with laudable and admirable steadfastness, did not want to bow down before the gentle breath of the great spirit.
>
> (p. 43)

Here Schleiermacher is surely advocating a particular religious attitude, resignation of the individual before the inevitable, however moral the individual's overridden aim and amoral the force that overrides it. It has nothing in common with the New Testament teaching that God's will is for the most part not done on Earth as it is in Heaven, and that we ought not to bow down and worship the World Spirit even though he has the kingdoms of the Earth at his disposal. However, my point here is not to criticise Schleiermacher for worshipping a god closer to Kali than to Jesus while being a minister of the Reformed Church, but simply to point out that thoroughly contentious beliefs are involved in his feeling for the universe.

This applies to morality too, even though his beliefs in this area are more congenial. He continues to distinguish religion from morality, but this is no longer the same difference that it was earlier in the speech. There he gave morality and religion honourable places side by side, one concerned with feeling, one with action. While the feeling/action contrast remains, this now differentiates two kinds of morality:

> Morals do not like love and affection, but activity, which proceeds wholly from within and is not produced by considering its external object; they know no other awe than that for their own law; they condemn as impure and self-seeking whatever can occur out of compassion and gratitude; they abuse, indeed despise, humility; and if you speak of remorse, they think of lost time that you unprofitably prolong.
>
> (p. 46)

But what he is speaking of here, with obvious distaste, is not morality as such, but Kantian morality; and in vindicating the feelings he mentions here as religion, he is vindicating a Spinozist (and indeed gospel) morality which teaches that if you get your emotions right, right action will look after itself. But Spinoza also taught that since emotions involve beliefs they can be more or less rational as those beliefs are more or less rational, and that the way to get better emotions is by getting truer beliefs. Schleiermacher's weakness here is not his Spinozism, but the fact that he is not more consistently Spinozist; it is not that he overstates the place of feeling in religion or in human life (he does not), but he treats feeling (sometimes) as non-cognitive, and therefore thinks (sometimes) that it can precede encounter with the word.

When in the fifth speech Schleiermacher comes to discuss the particular historical religions ('positive religion'), he surprises us by defending them rather than the 'natural religion' of the rationalists. Surely the historical religions get their different identities from their different doctrines? He thinks on the contrary that their differences merely reflect the individuality of different experiences of the universe. Yet if one has experiences about Christ or Krishna, that is surely only possible because one has heard and believed information about Christ or Krishna.

It may be useful in this connection to look at one positive religion which appears to make assumptions rather like Schleiermacher's about the relation between doctrine and experience, namely the Quakers. Quakers have a principled objection to doctrinal statements. Today this is often defended on the grounds of tolerance, but that was not the original reason. Seventeenth-century Quakers were no more tolerant than other sects, though they were tolerant about different things. The statutes of Pennsylvania were tolerant of different doctrines and forms of worship, but intolerant of unquakerly pastimes such as gambling. George Fox, while he certainly believed in civil liberty for all religions, did not show a tolerant attitude to other forms of worship or church organisation within Quakerism, and the Quakers have definite rules on these matters as much as they lack them about beliefs. But doctrine was regarded as secondary to experience. It is of course just as possible to be intolerant about forms of religious experience as about doctrines. I remember when many English evangelicals insisted that if you had not had a conversion experience preceded by a conviction of sin, and could not give a 'time when, place where and manner how', you were not a Christian. A curious thing about George Fox's journals is that he recounts the striking religious effect that his sermons had on their hearers, yet the content of the sermons seems to have been almost entirely negative: it is no use consulting priests or going to steeplehouse or taking sacraments or even reading the Bible. The modern secular reader is inclined to respond 'no, I never thought there was', but the hearers quaked at the word of the Lord and repented in tears. The point presumably is that none of these 'external' things is a substitute for the inner light of Christ. But this time surely it is the turn of those Fox was attacking, the Catholics and Presbyterians and Baptists, to say 'no, I never thought they were. But they are means of arousing an inner light of Christ'. Fox obviously felt that, far from being this, they were props which those with no experience of the inner light could cling to. Margaret Fell recounts how challenged she was by Fox's question: 'Thou sayest Christ says this and the apostles that, but what canst thou say?' It was no use, in other words, having the experience second hand. All of which has its point, but could Fox have had the experience first hand unless he had already heard of it second hand? When, after becoming disillusioned with all priests and steeplehouses, Fox finally found someone to speak to his condition, it is no accident that it was Christ, belief in whom Fox had been taught from his youth up. Nor is it an accident that the morality that the inner light of Christ revealed to Fox was a mixture of the one he had read in the Sermon on the Mount and the one he had imbibed from New Model Army radicalism.

Something similar can be said about the Quaker form of worship. Silence is maintained, outer and inner, so that God can speak. But this does not mean that some source of religious experience can be tapped by the simple expedient of keeping silent. Words are excluded from the worship, but the worship is surrounded by and set up by words: the words that announce that the building is a Meeting House of the Religious Society of Friends, that a Meeting for Worship will be held at 11 am; the words on the leaflet often handed out to newcomers to explain how the meeting works; the backlog of words in the worshippers' memories about the still, small voice speaking the word of God that was not in the earthquake, wind and fire, and so on. An analogy can be found in what the French Quaker Etienne Grellet said about the sacrament of communion, which as a Quaker he would no longer take; he said that ever since he had become a Quaker, whenever he ate bread and drank wine in the ordinary course of life, he thought of the body and blood of Christ. This expresses a genuine and lively religious consciousness, but one which could only exist because Grellet was familiar with the special sacramental use of bread and wine by other Christians. Likewise, undoctrinal Quakerism can only exist because doctrinal Christianity exists before it and around it, and can in some measure be taken for granted as known by Quakers.

## 2   The 'religious a priori'

If bare feeling will not get us anywhere, there is a view not far removed from it which will get us somewhere, though not (I will argue) to a non-cognitive account of faith. Granted that a religious emotion must be attached to some objects about which some beliefs must be held, could it not be that there is a sort of religious instinct which, like the Freudian instincts, only presents itself in the mind attached to the idea of some object, but which is flexible enough to be capable of attaching to virtually any object. Humankind, it has been said, is a worshipping animal; but we have worshipped plants and animals and heavenly bodies; the personified forces of sea and soil and weather, sex and war and wine-drinking; historical and legendary individuals; the Earth itself, the universe, and the maker of the universe. Could it not be argued that the instinct to worship is itself uncriticisable, and guarantees that we have some religion: the only question is, which?

It could be replied that some societies, for example modern capitalist Europe and to a lesser extent the 'communist' bloc, have existed without religion. But it is quite natural, even outside the contexts of the philosophy of religion or theological apologetics, to talk about money-worship and state-worship. Ex-theology-student Stalin catechised the Party with a vow to the dead Lenin; both Stalinism and commerce are highly iconoclastic in desecrating what is sacred to other religions, but so was Puritanism. Capitalism in particular has a blind faith in a Hidden Hand which makes all things work together for good to them that love money; it organises highly successful rituals (for instance, the national lottery) and of course, like Stalinism, has made more human sacrifices than any of the more traditional religions, even that of the Aztecs. They have no supernatural beings, of course, but neither does Theravada Buddhism; they have no afterlife, but neither does Biblical Judaism. Is it not more correct to say not that capitalism and Stalinism are irreligious, but that they worship false gods?

If we are to say this, we must make it clear whether we would regard any attitude as counting as secular. A certain kind of humanist, or an orthodox Marxist (a Trotskyist, for instance) or indeed a postmodernist, might agree that capitalism and Stalinism are religions, but mean that as a criticism, and claim secularity for their own world outlook. But Paul Tillich, for instance, who is one of the advocates of the 'religious a priori', would reply: whatever you place ultimate concern in is your god. It may (in the cases referred to) be human dignity, or human emancipation, or fashion. As Luther put it:

> A God is simply that whereon the human heart rests with trust, faith, hope, and love. If the resting is right, then the God is right; if the resting is wrong, then the God, too, is illusory.
> (*Commentary on the Book of Daniel*, quoted in R.B. Haldane *The Pathway to Reality*, vol. 2, p. 127)

Secularity would then mean having no ultimate concern. Yet, oddly, the nearest one can imagine to an attitude of no ultimate concern is a certain kind of Zen Buddhism (or in the West, Stoicism), which we commonly regard as a religious attitude.

Of course, proving that everyone is religious does rather weaken what is being claimed when you claim that anyone is religious. The price of making religion universal and cognitively contentless in this way is that everything comes to depend not on whether one is religious, but on what is one's religion. In the differences between religions, cognitive beliefs come into their own; and the religious a priori itself has not proved that the person who believes that only money matters is wrong, only that this view too shares something of religion: like St Paul, it redescribes covetousness as idolatry. As I have said, the religious a priori does get us somewhere: by redescribing mammon-worship and state-worship as religions, it removes the quite gratuitous sense of autonomy and superior rationality that often goes with secularism. But in itself the religious a priori does not give the basis for a religion; one could not work out a 'natural religion' using this as one's starting point. Rather, the religious a priori makes us receptive to the demands for worship which we contingently encounter. These can be from God as revealed in Jesus; they are more likely to be from the most powerful agencies existing in the society of the time, from Baal and Moloch (the names mean 'master' and 'king'), or from Mammon and the state.

So far from giving a non-cognitive account of religion, this view highlights the cognitive differences between religions. Far from making religious feeling enough, it makes it not even a beginning.

To conclude this chapter, pure feeling, that is feeling which does not itself presuppose and include beliefs, cannot be the foundation of religious beliefs. Emotions in the full sense involve beliefs; but then religious emotions can be felt only when one already has religious beliefs. They cannot be made the grounds of religious beliefs.

# 2  Faith without belief II

## Moral faith

I now turn to the two remaining conceptions of faith without belief, which interpret it as essentially a matter of moral commitment.

### 3  Kant: God as a postulate of practical reason

Now we come to the position which I think comes closest to being a coherent and worthy non-cognitive account of religion, that of Kant, on one reading of Kant (the 'as if' reading). I say on one reading, because there are three possible views which could be read into Kant. (i) If we take one crucial passage from the *Critique of Practical Reason* out of context, it looks as though Kant has an argument to prove the existence of God, a 'moral argument'. However, several things he says about this argument suggest the interpretation (ii) that it is not an argument for the existence of God, though it is an argument for believing in the existence of God. But this seems to me to be an untenable position between (i) and (iii), the idea that while we can't know whether God exists or not, we ought to act as if he did.

The argument (i) comes near the beginning of the section entitled 'The Existence of God as a Postulate of Pure Practical Reason' (Kant 1873, p. 221). It seems to have three premises which, while I do not necessarily accept them, are fairly plausible – and it does follow from them. There is nevertheless a flaw in the reasoning which I shall point out.

The three premises seem to be: (A) happiness ought to be proportioned to virtue (that is, the most virtuous person ought to be the happiest, and so on); (B) happiness cannot be proportioned to virtue unless there is a god to proportion them; and (C) 'ought' implies 'can'.

A is part of at least many people's moral 'commonsense'. We feel that it is unjust for a good person to suffer and a scoundrel to prosper. As Burns puts it:

It's hardly in a body's pow'r
To keep, at times, frae being sour,
To see how things are shar'd:
How best o' chiels are whiles in want,
While coofs [fools] on countless thousands rant,
And ken na how to wair't.
    ('Epistle to Davie', *Poems and Songs*, p. 14)

Kant points out that there is no necessary connection in this world between virtue and happiness, so that B holds. And in most contexts it seems pointless at least (Kant thinks, incoherent) to say that one ought to do things if one can't, so C seems plausible enough.

But then if happiness ought to be correlated to virtue, it follows that it can, and since it can't without a god to do the trick, there must be a god.

There is nothing wrong with the formal logic of this argument, but its formality obscures the way 'ought implies can' has to be used if it is to be at all plausible. It can't be used to prove that one can do something on the grounds that one ought to; it can only be used to prove that one has no obligation to do something which one can't. Otherwise, the following argument would also be valid: I ought to give a million pounds to the earthquake victims in Afghanistan; therefore I can give them a million pounds; so I am a millionaire! But I'm not.

What Kant should have concluded from 'ought implies can' together with the disproportion of virtue and happiness in this life is that, while it might be better if virtue and happiness were proportioned, there is no 'ought' about it.

In the following section Kant seems to backpedal a little, to position (ii). While still saying that theoretical reason is justified in assuming the postulates (including the existence of God) since they are practically necessary, he admits that 'speculative' (that is, theoretical) reason is not extended by these postulates, and that they are not cognitions, only 'thoughts in which there is nothing impossible' (Kant 1873, p. 232). In the *Critique of Pure Reason* he says:

my conviction is not *logical*, but *moral* certainty; and since it rests on subjective grounds (of the moral sentiment), I must not even say '*It is* morally certain that there is a God, etc.', but '*I am* morally certain, etc'.

(A829, B857)

But one can no more say 'it is not certain but I am certain of it' than one can say 'I believe it but it's not true'. One can say 'I *feel* certain' but that is not the same. Maybe the feeling of certainty is all Kant means here, since he goes on to say there is no cause for fear that belief in God could 'be taken from me'.

But it is necessary to distinguish between belief, practical determination and feeling if we are to avoid the self-deception of making ourselves believe what we think will help us, whether or not it is true.

If we do keep these things distinct, though, we arrive at the third reading of Kant: that we do not know whether there is a god or not, but we should act *as if* there is. Kant is not saying that we should act as if there is a god though there isn't; he is saying there is no impossibility about there being a god, but no proof that there is; and the moral life requires that we act on one of the two possibilities not the other: on the possibility that there is a god. This position could therefore be described as 'agnosticism of the intellect, theism of the will'. This has plenty of empirical parallels in secular life: occasions when we don't know which of two opinions is true, but have to act as if one is. In such circumstances we don't come to believe that the proposition which would justify the chosen alternative is true; we suspend judgement, but we don't suspend action, and this is entirely rational. For instance, the doctor prescribes medicines for the illness which he thinks explains my symptoms, though he knows it could be another illness; to judge that it was definitely one illness and not the other would be irrational, but so would failing to prescribe at all. Of course the doctor will not act exactly as he would if he was certain which illness I had; he will monitor my progress quite differently when uncertain than when certain. But he will probably prescribe the same medicine on the basis of guesswork that he would had he been certain.

Now the 'as if' account of 'moral faith', despite (or perhaps because of) its stark bleakness, has a certain nobility about it. It refuses any intellectually dishonest consolation, and will not deceive itself. It is willing to give itself the duties of a religious morality without any of the comforts. It combines a hard head and a pure heart. None of the criticisms of moral cowardice or intellectual slipperiness which can be made of some other non-cognitive accounts of faith apply here. One value of the 'as if' position is just that it shows up by contrast the irrationality of 'the will to believe'. I can only think of one religious thinker who has outdone even Kant in his commitment to well-doing without consolation: the author of *Ecclesiastes*, for whom there is neither any proportioning of virtue to happiness nor any permanence in our good work either here or hereafter, yet who tells us to work wholeheartedly, to fear God and to enjoy his earthly gifts:

> one fate comes to all, to the righteous and the wicked, to the good and the evil, to the clean and the unclean, to him who sacrifices and him who does not sacrifice. As is the good man, so is the sinner; and he who swears is as he who shuns an oath. This is an evil in all that is done under the sun, that one fate comes to all . . . But he who is joined with all the living has hope, for a living dog is better than a dead lion. For the living know that they will die, but the dead know nothing, and they have no more reward; but the memory of them is lost. Their love and their hate and their envy have already perished, and they have no more for ever any share in all that is done under the sun.
>
> Go, eat your bread with enjoyment, and drink your wine with a merry heart; for God has already approved what you do. Let your garments be always white; let not oil be lacking on your head. Enjoy life with the wife whom you love, all the days of your vain life which he has given you under the sun, because that is your portion in life and in your toil at which you toil under the sun. Whatever your hand finds to do, do it with your might; for there is no work or thought or knowledge or wisdom in Sheol, to which you are going.
>
> (ch. 9, vv. 2–10)

Despite the honesty and courage of Kant's position, there remains a question which it must answer if it is to make sense, and I am not convinced that it can. The question is: what is it to act as if there is a god? How does it differ from acting as if there were no god? Two obvious answers are not available to Kant: it might be thought that belief in God will bribe or scare us into doing what is right to gain rewards or avoid punishments hereafter; but such rightdoing would have no moral worth for Kant, since only what is done out of disinterested respect for the moral law has worth. And Kant also rejects the idea that the moral law is a set of arbitrary commands of God, which we would have no reason to obey had they not been commanded; the moral law is not right because God wills it, God wills it because it is right. So it is not something that only believers are committed to; it is equally binding on atheists. One might have a morality which depended on God in some other way than by being his edict. One example might be Augustine's morality, which enjoins first of all love of God, and then, as the consequence of this love, the ordered love of his creatures according to their degrees of being – people first, then animals, and so on. It is not clear how one could love God while doubting his existence, though, any more than while disbelieving in it. And as to the sublunary part of this morality (the duty of love to fellow creatures), either (a) the love of creatures stands or falls with the love of God, in which case there is a difference between acting as if God exists and acting as if he does not. But in this case it is not clear why it is better to act as if God exists than as if he does not, unless he does; for if he does not, some other morality will be better. Or (b) there are independent grounds for adhering to an ethic of the ordered love of beings, such as would be the sublunary part of Augustine's ethic. But in that case one will adhere to that ethic whether one believes in God or not, so nothing will count as acting as if God exists. And the same goes for any other moral position; if the existence of God makes a difference to how we should act, then there is no reason to act that way if he does not exist; if it doesn't make a difference, then nothing counts as acting as if he exists. The 'as if' position depends on two things: there being a difference between how we should act if God exists and how we should act if he doesn't, yet the former being better than the latter whether or not he exists. But you can't have it both ways – that combination is not possible.

It is only fair to discuss the difference that Kant himself thinks it makes. The point of God for Kant (rather like Robespierre's Supreme Being) is to match up virtue and happiness in the next life, since even the Revolutionary Tribunal can't get them properly matched here. But acting as if there were a god did not for Kant mean acting in fear of the Big Guillotine in the Sky, as we have seen. It seems to mean *working towards* the matching of virtue and happiness. However, there is nothing that we can do to match virtue and happiness in another life: either God does it, or it doesn't get done. And it is not even clear that we should try to match them on Earth: we haven't got a duty to go round doing favours for saints or kicking villains. But if it is a duty, it is not clear how the belief that the Celestial Committee for Public Safety will finish the job would influence how we do it. It might even stop us doing so on the grounds that 'vengeance is the Lord's'.

I conclude that there can be no moral ground for preferring one belief about the existence of God to another, unless it can be shown on independent grounds that God exists or does not. If it can, then if it is morally relevant at all which one believes, it will be better to believe the truth.

## 4   Braithwaite's fictionalism

I come now to an admirably clear analytical defence of non-cognitivism, R.B. Braithwaite's essay 'The Nature of Religious Belief' (reprinted in *The Philosophy of Religion*, ed. Basil Mitchell, Oxford University Press, 1971). Braithwaite starts with a logical positivist account of cognitive language. This would be an unpromising start for any cognitive account of religious belief, but I do not need to refute this (well-refuted) view here. Its relevance to the present argument is simply that it has the consequence that whatever religious belief might be, it must be non-cognitive.

Braithwaite's account of religious belief has four steps to it.

(i)   He adopts a prescriptivist view of moral language – that is to say, he holds moral principles to be essentially directions as to how to act. His emphasis differs from Hare's version of prescriptivism in being more 'first person': whereas Hare sees 'oughts' as commands directed to everyone, for Braithwaite to say that I ought to do something is to intend to do it. But Hare's prescriptivism also has that consequence, since to sincerely assent to a universal command is to commit oneself to obeying it; and since Braithwaite also thinks that this intention must be generalisable, the two views are essentially the same.

> What is the reason for my doing what I think I ought to do? The answer [this view] gives is that, since my thinking that I ought to do the action is my intention to do it if possible, the reason why I do the

action is simply that I intend to do it, if possible. On every other ethical view there will be a mysterious gap to be filled somehow between the moral judgement and the intention to act in accordance with it: there is no such gap if the primary use of a moral assertion is to declare such an intention.

(p. 79)

Whether this view does not leave an equally mysterious gap in accounting for the intention is a question that he does not consider.

(ii)   He claims that religious language is essentially moral language, with the proviso that religious assertions form a system and thus prescribe a way of life, not just a moral rule:

> the intention of a Christian to follow a Christian way of life is not only the criterion for the sincerity of his belief in the assertions of Christianity; it is the criterion for the meaningfulness of his assertions.
>
> To say that it is belief in the dogmas of religion which is the cause of the believer's intending to behave as he does is to put the cart before the horse: it is the intention to behave which constitutes what is known as religious conviction.
>
> (p. 80)

But this so far gives no way of distinguishing religion from any moral way of life, however secular. So Braithwaite draws our attention to two further features.

(iii)   The conversion involved in accepting a religion is a conversion, not only of the will, but of the heart. Christianity requires not only that you should behave towards your neighbour as if you loved him as yourself: it requires that you should love him as yourself.

(p. 83)

However, this is still not enough to differentiate different religions (e.g. Judaism, Christianity, Buddhism, if all 'agapeistically' interpreted – that is, interpreted as ethics of love), and indeed, until Kant, and aside from the Stoics, few secular moralists envisaged the sort of dislocation of 'will' from emotions that is rejected here. The identifying feature of a given religion – what distinguishes Judaism, Christianity and Buddhism – is specified by the final point.

> (iv)  The intentions to pursue the behaviour policies, which may be the same for different religions, are associated with thinking of different *stories* (or sets of stories). By a story I shall mean here a proposition or set of propositions which are straightforwardly empirical propositions capable of empirical test . . .
>
> A religious assertion will, therefore, have a propositional element which is lacking in a purely moral assertion, in that it will refer to a story as well as to an intention. The reference to the story is not an assertion of the story as a matter of empirical fact: it is a telling of the story, or an alluding to the story, in the way in which one can tell, or allude to, the story of a novel with which one is acquainted.
>
> (p. 84)

This, it seems to me, gives the whole non-cognitive game away. For if prescriptive language can really stand on its own as non-cognitive ethics states, what use are stories, which are cognitive – indeed propositional – in form? Braithwaite's answer is that they are causally conducive of the morality that they are associated with:

> the relation is a psychological and causal one. It is an empirical psychological fact that many people find it easier to resolve upon and carry through a course of action which is contrary to their natural inclinations if this policy is associated in their minds with certain stories.
>
> (p. 86)

Now anyone who accepts a cognitive theory of ethics will have a clear account of how 'stories' affect behaviour, and this will not be a matter of some purely fortuitous causal link; the account will be: rational behaviour is a function of the person's (cognitive) beliefs. If we think it true that God loves us, we may love God in return, and love our fellow creatures as a consequence. A fiction may also have some such effect, but whether it does or not will depend on the verisimilitude that we attribute to that fiction. Nicholas Berdyaev was drawn to Christianity by the image of Christ in Dostoevsky's Legend of the Grand Inquisitor, but presumably this would not have resulted in his conversion had he not believed that the real Christ was of like character to Dostoevsky's fiction about him.

But Braithwaite takes a different view:

> it is not necessary, on my view, for the asserter of a religious assertion to believe in the truth of the story involved in the assertions: what is necessary is that the story should be entertained in thought.
>
> (pp. 85–6)

But if the stories are not meant to be true, or at least illustrative of the sort of thing that is true, how do they affect the person's actions? The *intelligible, internal* relation that subsists between a belief and the actions which it makes rational is removed, and a brute causal one substituted: maybe people behave in a more loving way after hearing a given story, but if that is not because they believe in the truth or verisimilitude of the story, then that fact is no more significant than if they behave in a more loving way after smoking cannabis. Braithwaite tells us:

> it is *all* the thoughts of a man that determine his behaviour; and these include his phantasies, imaginations, ideas of what he would wish to be and do, as well as the propositions which he believes to be true.
>
> (p. 87)

And he calls this 'a commonplace to all students of the influence of literature upon life'. But any account of how this happens which is to show an intelligible link between story and action will have to show how literature alters our beliefs. This may include beliefs about what is possible as well as about what is actual, but possibilities are as much a real feature of the world about which we can have objective knowledge as are actualities. Of course, literature may affect one causally other than through beliefs – a tedious novel may make you bored or an erotic one may cause sexual arousal. But clearly that is not how the Legend of the Grand Inquisitor in *The Brothers Karamazov* affected Berdyaev. Rather, it is a matter of believing that Christ's understanding of the human condition as there presented is the true one, and the Grand Inquisitor's false; and that the understanding exemplified by Christ in the novel is also the understanding revealed by the real Christ's life on Earth.

However, Braithwaite disavows that the connection between story and action is internal anyway:

> My contention . . . has the great advantage of imposing no restriction whatever upon the empirical interpretation which can be put upon the stories.
>
>     . . . there is no action which is appropriate to thinking of a proposition without believing it; thinking of it may, as I have said, produce a state of mind in which it is easier to carry out a particular course of action, but the connection is causal: there is no intrinsic connection between the thought and the action.[1]
>
> (p. 88)

But in the first place, if we can interpret the stories how we like they really no longer differentiate different religions: consider the way a Satanist might read the story of the fall or of Christ's temptation, or less fantastically how an orthodox Jew might read the stories of the confrontations between Jesus and the Pharisees. In fact, all religions include interpretations of their stories as well as the stories themselves and the codes of conduct that they motivate. Indeed, it should by now not be necessary to point out that there is no hard and fast line between a story and its interpretation. And in the case of the Gospels, it is clear enough that the interpretation largely came before them and explained the events they described, in Deutero-Isaiah's conception of the Messiah as suffering servant of Yahweh.

And if there is no fit – no appropriateness or intrinsic connection – between story and action, then it seems that any story which does the trick will do. The irreplaceability of particular stories for particular religions becomes no more than an irrational prejudice. Why read the Gospels if one can promote 'agapeistic' behaviour as effectively by *The Wizard of Oz*? Aside from its inherent irrationalism, this view will certainly not stand as an account of how Christians have historically understood the stories they told. The apostles did not think of their 'good news' in the way that Plato thought of his 'noble lie'.

Finally, there is the awkward fact that one participant in these stories told by theistic religions (empirically verifiable as Braithwaite supposes them to be) is *God*. Braithwaite accommodates this in the way common to post-Kantian liberal Protestantism by reducing talk of God to talk of doing the will of God:

one story common to all the moral theistic religions which has proved
of great psychological value in enabling religious men to persevere in
carrying out their religious behaviour policies – the story that in doing
so they are doing the will of God.

(p. 88)

In order to drive a wedge between this story and the behaviour it
motivates, he points out that 'the intention to do what a person [God]
desires or commands, irrespective of what this command or desire may be,
is no part of a higher religion' (pp. 88–9). Although there have in fact been
philosophers – whether they belong to 'higher religion' or not – who have
thought that the arbitrary command of God was the foundation of religious
morality (Ockham, Kierkegaard and Wittgenstein, for instance),
Braithwaite is right to reject that view. But this is not the only way in
which belief in God could be intrinsically related to the works of love to
which it gives rise. For the Christians most worthy of imitation, God does
not enter the 'story' by revealing arbitrary commands, but by revealing his
love for us. The revelation that God loves us and gives himself for us is
the ground of our love for him, which in turn is the ground for what
Braithwaite calls an 'agapeistic way of life'. The statement 'God is love'
does not just (does not even) 'declare' the intention to follow such a way
as Braithwaite thinks (p. 81); it motivates it. Otherwise the second of
Jesus's two greatest commandments (to love one's neighbour as oneself)
would stand in no need of the first (to love God), and the first would stand
in no need of the knowledge that God is love, which we should never have
known but for his self-revelation in Jesus Christ.

In short, the link between the statement 'God is love' and living
'agapeistically' is neither a logical relation of meaning (as Braithwaite
seems to suggest on p. 81), nor an accidental causal relation (as he seems
to conclude later), but an intelligible causal relation with an intermediate
link in the causal chain: loving God. And one can't love God unless one
believes that he exists.

Braithwaite's account of Christian belief does not answer the question
how propositions are connected with actions in Christianity. What it
answers is the question how much of Christian belief one could retain
while being an atheist or an agnostic. For it is certainly possible to derive
inspiration from the gospel story and adhere to the prescriptive part of the
New Testament while being an atheist. It may not be a rationally

defensible position, but it is a really instantiated one. But to describe such a person as a Christian is misleading; one might as well describe Marx as a Greek pagan because he drew inspiration from the legend of Prometheus.

Both Kant and Braithwaite are clearly reducing religion to something else, to morality, or morality plus some decorative extra. For many thinkers of the Enlightenment and the nineteenth century this seemed a defence of religion: morality was accepted as an absolute; if Christianity was simply morality at its best, who could reject it? There were always dissident voices: if morality is Christianity, said William Blake, then Socrates is saviour. Blake recognised not only that reducing Christianity to mere morality was an impoverishment of its heritage, but that morality is not an absolute: that if you pursue morality for its own sake, as Kant urges, you will become not a saint, but at best a self-divided person, at worst a self-righteous hypocrite. The last word of Christianity about morality is: love God truly, and morality will look after itself. There is a similar idea in the Taoist classic *Tao Te Ching*. I don't know if it can be found in other religions. But so far as Christianity is concerned, its reduction to morality does not just take away what is distinctive about it as a religion, it destroys its distinctive view of morality too.

# 3 Non-cognitive grounds for belief

Leaving accounts of faith which try to portray it without any belief content, we come to views which recognise that faith involves belief but think that it can be justified without any cognitive grounds for that belief – that is, even when there is nothing to support the claim that the belief is true. Belief is seen as quite legitimately being the result of choice or self-persuasion, or a 'leap in the dark' – or simply as needing no reasons. I shall consider four versions of this view.

## 1 Pascal's wager

Pascal, the mathematician who invented probability theory in response to a gambler's puzzle, sees the choice between (Catholic) belief and unbelief as a bet. As in any fair bet, we do not know the outcome of the game in advance:

> 'Either God exists, or He does not.' To which view shall we incline? Reason cannot decide for us one way or the other.
>
> (*Pensées*, p. 93)

Can we then refuse to bet, and suspend judgement? Pascal says not: 'a bet must be laid. There is no option: you have joined the game' (p. 94).

Pascal does not say why, but it could be simply that God will not take 'I don't know' for an answer, that agnosticism as much as atheism will lead to Hell. This would avoid the philosophical retort that a Kantian 'as if' is an option, but would incur the guilt of persuading by threatening. However, I repeat, Pascal does not say this here; indeed, Hell is not mentioned in the entire wager argument.

Since the odds are level, Pascal argues, the rational person will look at the stakes. What you bet is finite (one lifespan). What you stand to gain is infinite – an eternity of happiness. So it is reasonable to bet on God – indeed would be however bad the odds.

To the objection that one is not free to choose to believe, he argues that it is one's passions that prevent one from believing; act so as to subdue them, and you will be able to believe. There follows the notorious passage:

> Learn of those who were once bound and gagged like you, and who now stake all that they possess. They are men who know the road that you desire to follow, and who have been cured of a sickness of which you desire to be cured. Follow the way by which they set out, acting as if they already believed, taking holy water, having masses said, etc. Even this will naturally cause you to believe, and blunt your cleverness.
>
> (p. 95)

Pascal is not guilty of the philosophical error (as I will argue it to be) of claiming that we can believe by choosing to do so. Rather, he is saying (what is true) that if we act in certain ways (holy water, masses) we may come to believe. But what this seems at first sight to be recommending is something not so much philosophically incoherent as morally dishonest: deliberate self-deception, a programme of self-indoctrination at the end of which we will have firm beliefs which we knew to be doubtful at the beginning. The reference to blunting your cleverness suggests what one might call (parodying Kant) self-stupefaction with immoderate quantities of holy water.

However, at this point in his argument, Pascal seems to see it rather differently from this: he sees our passions as the reasons we do not believe, which presumably we otherwise would; it is not the holy water that deceives us into believing – rather our passions make us deceive ourselves into unbelief. Holy water and masses are seen as ways of removing these irrational obstacles to belief. One could reconstruct a version of this last point of Pascal's which does not involve self-deception and avoids the implausible reliance on holy water. Suppose one were to say: if you can't love God because you are unsure of his existence, try loving other beings better; your neighbours, the oppressed of the Earth, even your enemies – and nature as well as humankind. Try loving them seriously, overcoming your resentment and greed for the sake of this love. The scales will fall from your eyes, and you will experience the presence of God.

This last point of Pascal's argument then – the part that has caused most offence – is not necessarily as unworthy as it is often seen. Nor is *this* part a case for belief on non-cognitive grounds at all: the grounds when you get them will be cognitive. Only to get them you first have to undergo a (non-cognitive) discipline – but one that is admirable in itself. Of course, the proof of this pudding remains in the eating – and it is not an easy diet to follow.

But this does not rescue the wager argument as a whole. Firstly, because while at the end Pascal is blaming unbelief on passions, he has earlier admitted that the limits of reason are the grounds for doubt; secondly, because, even though he is not explicitly threatening us with hellfire, he is bribing us with happiness hereafter. If we serve God it should surely be because we love God, not because we want a reward. We ought to love God as the author of *Ecclesiastes* loved him. Thirdly, there is no reason given why we should not respond to the uncertainty by suspending cognitive judgement and betting only practically, like Kant. After all, a real gambler does not necessarily *believe* his horse will win. I have suggested that Pascal may think the Kantian option won't do because God will not accept it, but this would be a retreat to arbitrariness and threats. Finally, Pascal only considers the options of atheism and Catholicism. Aside from the fact that this rests on the accident of his birth in seventeenth-century France, it allows anyone willing to adopt a barbaric enough religion to trump the argument: 'if you worship Woden, you will get infinite pleasure in Valhalla without sacrificing it here; and if you don't worship Woden, you will get infinitely more pain in Hel than you would in Hell. So on the same principles that led you to prefer Catholicism to atheism, you must now get down on your knees before Woden.' In short, whatever religion could offer the biggest sticks and carrots would convert the most donkeys. It is the otherworldly egoism that brings Pascal's argument down; philosophically, it is stronger than the next argument I shall consider.

## 2   The will to believe

Although the idea that you can choose to believe something is often attributed to Pascal, William James is the clearest case of a philosopher who actually believed not just that one could make choices which would eventually result in one's believing, but that one could believe just by choosing. James was familiar with Pascal's argument, which he rejects, as I have, not so much on philosophical as on moral grounds:

> You probably feel that when religious faith expresses itself thus, in the language of the gaming table, it is put to its last trumps . . . we feel that a faith in masses and holy water adopted wilfully after such a mechanical calculation would lack the inner soul of faith's reality; and if we were ourselves in the place of the Deity, we should probably take particular pleasure in cutting off believers of this pattern from their infinite reward.
>
> (*Essays in Popular Philosophy*, p. 6)

(Though mixed with the objection to afterworldly self-interest here there is doubtless some Protestant prejudice against masses and holy water, and indeed against gaming tables.)

Although James was a pragmatist, who thought that ultimately truth itself was definable in practical terms, he by no means thought that you could believe just whatever suited you. Several conditions are necessary before the will to believe can come into play. But first I must mention three preliminary arguments of James's, though I shall not take them in the same order as he does, since they are somewhat mixed in the text and I want to treat them separately.

Firstly, he points out that we do often, in fact, believe things without good cognitive grounds because we want to. This is certainly true but does not get us any nearer to the will to believe, since not only is such wishful thinking the paradigm case of irrationality, but it is also only possible if done unwittingly. If the Pascalian gambler went to mass and took holy water saying 'here I am fooling myself into believing that there is a god', he would never succeed.

Secondly, James points out that it is no more rational to disbelieve something on slender evidence than to believe it on slender evidence. When Clifford says 'It is wrong always, everywhere, and for every one, to believe anything on insufficient evidence' (quoted p. 8), he is not advocating rationality but undue scepticism, for rationality issues two maxims: 'Believe truth! Shun error!' (p. 18) and Clifford is urging us to pursue the latter at the expense of the former. It is no worse to believe what is false through undue gullibility than to disbelieve what is true through undue scepticism. All this is true and important. But it does not establish any will to believe. When you believe something with 90 per cent probability, you are not choosing to believe, but proportioning belief to evidence (for the belief will not, as I shall argue, be the same as belief based on 100 per cent probability).

Thirdly, James mentions cases in which one has to believe something in order to make it true, for instance believing that someone is your friend may be necessary in order for the friendship to develop. I shall discuss this in connection with Bultmann in the next section, since it is more relevant to his main argument than to James's.

Now we come to the conditions of the possibility of the will to believe. In the first place, James is as aware as anyone that there is no place in science for wishful thinking or any kind of subjective judgement. The will to believe only comes into play where there are no compelling intellectual reasons for opting one way or the other. James has it in common with Pascal and Kant that he holds this to be the case with religious belief. In addition to this, the will to believe can only operate when (i) the options chosen between are live options; (ii) the choice is a forced one, i.e. one cannot avoid choosing; and (iii) the issue is momentous, not trivial. There are no particular philosophical problems about the third point, but there are about the other two. The notion of a live option is intuitively clear enough; most people can imagine themselves adopting one of a variety of mutually incompatible views, but there will always be other views that one cannot imagine oneself adopting. In this sense, for instance, Christianity and dialectical materialism are live options for me, but Islam and liberalism are not. This is not a matter of which options are attractive: I can think of few religions more attractive than polytheism, and if I had no constraints but my own choice on what I should worship, I would probably worship trees. But these are not live options.

But a few points need clearing up about live and dead options. First of all, the admission that one has more than one live option does not mean by itself that one can choose between them and so has a will to believe; it means that one can imagine choosing between them. Something would have to happen, though, to make the choice compelling. Secondly, there are typically two reasons why options that are live for one person may be dead for another. It may be a case of cultural alienness; or it may be that one has good cognitive grounds for believing a view false, or no grounds for believing it true. In the former case, greater cultural understanding can make live options out of previously dead ones, and indeed thousands of English people with a Christian or secular background now find Buddhism or Islam or Vedanta live options, just as thousands of Indians now find Christianity a live option – none of which things were true in 1800. But something can also be made a live – or dead – option by arguments being presented for or against it. Cognitive grounds do not only come into play when an option is already live.

Now we come to the crucial point: the idea that the choice for or against religion is a forced option. A Kantian holding the 'as if' interpretation of Kant might say that there is a third option, namely acting as if religion is true (or indeed false) while suspending judgement about it intellectually. The example that James gives to show that suspending judgement can be equivalent to rejecting something is that of marriage, but the point about marriage is that it is a practical step and therefore, however many reservations one has about it, one has to take a decision; deciding to marry a particular person does not entail losing all such reservations, and many people marry despite continuing to have them. It is by assimilating 'choice' of belief to choice of action that James rules out suspension of judgement; but suspension of judgement does not rule out choice of action, as Kant's position shows. One can easily think of secular parallels: suppose you are escaping from enemy troops in a war and the only escape route lies across an unsafe bridge spanning a deep ravine. Do you cross the bridge and risk plunging to your death, or do you await the certainty of capture and uncertainty of treatment at the enemies' hands? You cannot avoid decision. But whatever you decide, you will not come to believe that it is completely safe; if you cross the bridge you will not dance merrily across, but take the greatest of care. You will in one sense be acting 'as if' the bridge were safe, but the 55 per cent chance which you give it will come out in your behaviour as well as your thoughts and feelings. Nothing about the forced nature of practical decisions forces beliefs: I have met a Catholic philosopher who thought there was a serious, though less than 50 per cent, chance that Christianity is false, and a secular philosopher who thought that there is a serious, though less than 50 per cent chance, that it is true. I do not regard either as irrational, or even unusual.

The crucial argument against James, though, is that if someone claims to have a belief which they know is the result of choice not evidence, they are simply misdescribing their own experience; it cannot be a belief, for knowing that it is a result of choice, they cannot think they know it, for a belief's being knowledge involves there being good grounds for it; and to believe is to claim to know. All the Jamesian 'believer' really has is a will to make-believe.

## 3  Bultmann's *kerygma*

Braithwaite's philosophical commitment to logical positivism makes it impossible for him to give an account of Christianity that is genuinely theistic; Bultmann, though a theologian by training, is also deeply committed to a philosophical position, and one which in many respects is as far removed as it could be from logical positivism, namely Heidegger's variety of existentialism. Bultmann is often accused of simply taking over Heidegger's thought and rewriting the New Testament in terms of it. However, this overlooks two facts: that the dialogue between Bultmann and Heidegger while they were colleagues at Marburg took place before and during the composition of Heidegger's *Being and Time*, and it is probable that the influence was not all one way; certainly, Heidegger was at this time profoundly influenced by Luther's reading of the New Testament. And secondly, that the influence of Kant on Bultmann as on all liberal Protestant theology was profound, and Bultmann's project of 'demythologisation' of the Christian message is more Kantian than Heideggerian in its assumption. To this point I shall return.

Neither Kant's philosophy nor Heidegger's rules out theism in the way that logical positivism does, and Bultmann's position is clearly theistic. As we should expect of a Protestant and a Kantian, he rules out natural theology. But we are concerned here with his non-cognitive account of revealed theology. I believe that two things will emerge from this discussion: (i) that while Bultmann wants to give a non-cognitive account of revelation, he always slips either into talking about some other kind of event than revelation or into talking about a tacitly cognitive revelation; (ii) that he wants to show that revelation is something more than objective knowledge in that it affects us in the depths of our personal lives, but he nowhere shows us either why objective knowledge cannot so affect us, nor how revelation can without being (believed to be) objective knowledge. In the end, revelation turns out to be either a kind of objective knowledge after all, or else something not more but less than objective knowledge.

In his essay 'Revelation in the New Testament' (in *Existence and Faith*) Bultmann distinguishes concepts of revelation as '*communication of knowledge by the word*' and as '*an occurrence that puts me in a new situation as a self*'. What, though, is such an occurrence? An occurrence of this kind could *consist in* the communication of knowledge by the word, so the two are not, as Bultmann seems to suppose, mutually exclusive. Bultmann gives the following examples:

> In a crime, for example, there is 'revealed' to me the abyss of man's nature; and in the death of a friend there is 'revealed' to me something of what dying means. Through an experience my 'eyes are opened' about myself – say, about my weakness or my unscrupulousness. One person 'reveals' himself to another through an act of friendship or love and also through an act of hate or meanness.
>
> (p. 68)

But these examples are clearly things which 'communicate knowledge', whether by the word or by 'direct' experience. If a non-cognitive version of revelation is to be illustrated, a more plausible example, which Bultmann uses elsewhere, would be making a new friendship or falling in love. These really are 'occurrences that put me in a new situation as a self', other than by giving me new information. But one must know someone in order to befriend or fall in love with them. Of course this will be 'knowledge by acquaintance' rather than 'knowledge by description'. But this last distinction can't be the one that Bultmann is trying to make. For quite apart from anything else, knowledge of *Christ* can, for those of us who come after, only be knowledge by description in the first instance. Even if we have as direct experience of Christ as Paul did on the Damascus road, we can do so only because we have already heard about him. 'Faith comes by hearing, and hearing by the word of God' (Romans 10.17). Bultmann would be the first to recognise this, but he still seeks to avoid a cognitive account of revelation by his notion of the word as *kerygma*, as we shall see. Thus

> If preaching communicates a content, it at the same time addresses us; it speaks to our consciences, and whoever refuses to let himself be addressed likewise does not understand what is communicated.
>
> (p. 91)

But what is it that addresses us if not the content communicated, and how can we refuse to let it address us except by ignoring, or disbelieving, the content communicated? Yet Bultmann always wants to drive a wedge between the truth content and the existential pull, what is said and what is done by the saying. He never succeeds in showing how saying something can do something other than by virtue of what is said.

> From the outside, there is no way to discover what in human speech is God's Word. *God's Word is always summons* and is understood as God's Word only when the summons is understood and *heard* in the real sense of the word. Therefore God's Word has no authentication; it demands recognition. From a neutral standpoint, it cannot be understood as God's Word.
>
> ('The Word of God in the New Testament',
> in *Faith and Understanding*, p. 300)

Aside from the fact that the New Testament takes authentication very seriously, three points need to be made about this passage.

(1) An unauthenticated word which demands recognition is an authoritarian word in the bad sense. It is not always bad or irrational to accept a word on authority, but that is because some authorities are authenticated. I take my doctor's advice because I believe him to be a well-trained and skilful physician. Unauthenticated demands for recognition leave us no grounds for discerning the good from the evil authorities.

(2) The first and last sentences of the last quote suggest that God's word can only speak to those who already accept it. Are we talking about preaching to the converted? Surely the *kerygma* was addressed precisely to those outside, to those neutral or indeed hostile.

(3) A summons could be a simple imperative, and the origin of the New Testament term *kerygma* as meaning a heraldic proclamation even suggests this: 'get out of the Emperor's way!' But in fact the New Testament *kerygma* is never like that; it is always in the indicative, or else

its imperatives are backed by indicatives. The contrast between 'word as communication' and 'word as address or summons' is a false one. The word addresses or summons us only by communicating something. It is only because the 'summons' or *kerygma* is referred to emptily here that it could seem otherwise. As soon as we give content to the *kerygma*, for instance Peter's Pentecost sermon (Acts 2.22–36) we see that the *kerygma* contains a great deal of information. And if 'when they heard this they were cut to the heart', that is for no other reason than that the knowledge communicated by Peter's sermon was powerfully disturbing stuff. It was not an effect of some other quality of the preaching than what it communicated. Statements like

> just as little as the proclamation communicates something that happened in a certain place and at a certain time, but rather says what has occurred to the person being addressed, so little is faith the knowledge of some fact within the world, or the willingness to hold some remarkable dogma to be true
>
> (*Existence and Faith*, p. 101)

cannot account for Peter's sermon, or any other sermon in the New Testament. Of course faith is not *just* knowledge of some fact, but trust in a person; but that trust logically presupposes, and is rationally motivated by, knowledge about that person. Bultmann seems unable to envisage the possibility that objective knowledge can change one's existence. Like Braithwaite, he believes in a cognitively ungrounded 'act of will' as the basis of conversion and faith. Yet unlike Braithwaite, he is a theist. As a result, he holds an odd combination of views. On the one hand, he accepts the objection against the 'subjectivising' tendency of older liberal theology, that 'faith has real meaning only if God exists outside the believer' (*Jesus Christ and Mythology*, p. 70). On the other hand, he rejects the idea that the believer could have any grounds outside him- or herself for believing that this is so.

> Thus, the fact that God cannot be seen or apprehended apart from faith does not mean that He does not exist apart from faith.
>
>     We must remember, however, that the affirmation of faith in relation to its object, to God, cannot be proved objectively. . . .

May we then say that God has 'proved' Himself by the 'facts of redemption' (*Heilstatsachen*)? By no means. For what we call facts of redemption are themselves objects of faith and are apprehended as such only by the eye of faith. They cannot be perceived apart from faith, as if faith could be based on data which are open to empirical observation.

*(Jesus Christ and Mythology*, p. 72)

The reading of this passage is complicated by the ambiguity of 'faith' between 'belief' and 'trust'. Certainly, the faith which saves is trust, not mere belief. 'The devils also believe, and tremble' (James 2.19). But on the one hand, trust presupposes belief: an agnostic cannot trust God. And on the other hand, there is no ground for trust in God unless we believe that the 'facts of redemption' actually occurred, and really were the acts of God. And if we do have these beliefs, then trust is the rational consequence. So we have to establish that belief is in order before we can talk about trust.

However, Bultmann seems to be saying, or at least implying, that we should believe in something while also believing that there are no grounds for that belief. And that is impossible. To say 'God has acted, but there is no reason for me or anyone to believe so' is self-undermining; for to say that something is so is also to stand warranty for there being good reasons to hold that it is. To believe something is to hold that there are good grounds for believing it, even though one may not be able to state what they are. And if it is belief (rather than trust) which is at issue, it does not help to say that it has its grounds in itself: 'the facts of redemption constitute the grounds of faith, but only as perceived by faith itself' (*ibid.*). However, what Bultmann may be doing here is denying what I have just said about trust presupposing belief:

Trust in a friend can rest solely on the personality of my friend which I can perceive only when I trust him. There cannot be any trust or love without risk.

(pp. 72–3)

But we do in fact always know something of a person before we trust them as a friend. We do not of course have proof, in the sense of a valid deductive argument from indubitable premisses, either for the trustworthiness of a friend, or the existence of God, or any other proposition outside mathematics. Nor, unless we are churlish, do we demand 'proofs of friendship'. And so trusting a friend involves risk, as does trusting in God, or eating a sandwich (it might be infected with salmonella) or turning on the light (there might have been a gas leak), or anything else we do. But it does not follow that trusting a friend is an arbitrary act or a leap in the dark. We may well not be able to spell out what draws us to a friend – but it is when we have started to get to know them that something does.

Now it is certainly the aim of Christian life that one should 'find a friend in Jesus'. Whatever may have been the case for Peter and John and Mary Magdalen, we cannot do that in the same way as we make friends with our earthly contemporaries. We begin with the word. Only when we have learnt to know him by description from the New Testament can we get to know him personally, and only insofar as we know him can we know the Father (for if we proceed from our knowledge of this world to knowledge of a god, we arrive only at the god of this world, who in New Testament teaching is a different personage altogether).

The analogy of friendship seems to be meant to suggest that Bultmann's 'faith' is something non-cognitive – some sort of trust which does not presuppose belief, though it may lead to it. However, Bultmann does not consistently present revelation or the *kerygma* as without cognitive content. Thus he tells us: 'revelation consists in nothing other than the fact of Jesus Christ. His coming as such is designated as the revelation' (*Existence and Faith*, p. 87). Yet he straightway qualifies this: 'it is now a *veiled revelation*'. This looks like not non-cognitive belief, but cognitive belief without cognitive grounds: realism about God, irrationalism about belief in him.

If the 'summons' of the *kerygma* gives us no grounds for its claims on us, and refuses the demand for authentication, why should we obey this summons rather than those others that confront us? That Bultmann held fast to his faith when so many others were following the summons of Hitler is a credit to his courage. But can he tell us why that decision was right? (One may turn to his critique of Kamlah in his essay 'The New Testament and Mythology' in *Kerygma and Myth*, pp. 25ff., to read how he tries to do so; it is in terms of the incapacity of fallen humankind to save itself. But this makes it look as though the issue turns on a matter of anthropology, rather than faith.)

Part of the appeal of non-cognitive accounts of Christian belief in an age in which that belief is on the defensive is that it reassures Christians who have come to doubt the cognitive grounds for their beliefs that they may go on being Christians with a good intellectual conscience. But it does so at a price: that of abandoning the claim to be able to give the non-believer grounds for believing.

I have traced Bultmann's attempt to empty the *kerygma* of its cognitive content to a (false) philosophical position: the prejudice common among existentialists that objective knowledge cannot affect us in our being, cannot 'cut us to the heart'. But there is another motive as well: Bultmann's scepticism about the historical event in which God's revelation in Christ took place – about, for instance, the messianic claims of Jesus, and his resurrection. He accepts it as beyond serious doubt that Jesus existed, preached the coming of the Kingdom of God, and was crucified; he regards this as enough historical basis for the *kerygma*. But in the first place, if the *kerygma* does not communicate knowledge, why is even this historical basis necessary? Why not just say: 'repent!'? And in the second place, if Peter had simply said 'there was a man called Jesus who preached the kingdom of God and was crucified', no one would have been cut to the heart. More objective knowledge was needed for that to happen.

However, what I have said about Bultmann so far could mislead the reader. For Bultmann often says things about faith carrying with it its own understanding, and even about the imperative in the *kerygma* being based on the indicative. This certainly shows that he does not advocate a non-cognitive faith. Does he really, as I am claiming, believe in faith without cognitive grounds?

The first thing to say here is that, as a follower of Heidegger, Bultmann believes that human existence involves three 'existentialia' (fundamental concepts for understanding human existence), namely understanding (the cognitive one), state-of-mind (*Befindlichkeit*, the emotive one), and discourse. Also, that while these three are analytically distinguishable, they always come together: there is no understanding without a state-of-mind or state-of-mind without an understanding, and so on. But it seems to me that for Bultmann the understanding that comes with faith *follows* from faith, rather than the other way round. Trust leads to belief rather than belief leading to trust. This is shown by his habitual contrasting of faith with proof, despite what he has written about faith elsewhere. For

Bultmann has written well and illuminatingly about the New Testament concept of faith (*pistis*) in his *Theology of the New Testament* and his entry on faith in Kittel's Theological Dictionary. He emphasises the notions of trust and obedience in *pistis*, and doesn't confuse it with unreasoned belief. But then, by contrasting it with proof, he falls victim to precisely that confusion. If faith is trust, then a proof that God is love is a ground for faith, not an alternative to it.

## 4    Basic beliefs: Plantinga

The last example of a theory of belief without cognitive grounds that I shall look at is that put forward by Alvin Plantinga in his paper 'Is Belief in God Rational?'. It is unlike the others in several respects. In the first place, it does not attribute belief to some non-cognitive 'faculty', such as feeling or will; and it is certainly about belief in a cognitive sense, not something less than cognitive. Yet it defends the rationality of belief in God as *basic*, in the sense of having no other beliefs as its grounds and, I take it, having no experiences or arguments as its grounds either.

The argument is an anti-foundationalist one: foundationalists are described as treating certain kinds of proposition as basic, and others as only rational if evidenced by basic propositions. Basic beliefs are basic in that they are not based on any other beliefs; for the foundationalist, they are generally beliefs which are either incorrigible as based on immediate sensation, or self-evident in the way that simple propositions of logic and mathematics are. Immediate sensations are said to be incorrigible in that one cannot be wrong about having a pain in the back or seeming to smell lavender, though one may be wrong about one's claim to have a slipped disc or to be smelling lavender. $2 + 2 = 4$ is said to be self-evident in that one can 'just see' – supposedly infallibly – that it is true. The foundationalist typically holds that a person's noetic structure – their set of beliefs and the mutual relations between those beliefs – is rational only if the basic beliefs in it are self-evident or incorrigible, and the other beliefs founded on them. But this belief of the foundationalists can itself hardly be either self-evident or incorrigible, or even founded on beliefs that are.

I think Plantinga is quite right to reject this foundationalist position. As Kenny points out in a discussion which takes off from Plantinga's (and which I will discuss more fully later),[1] many beliefs which are clearly neither self-evident nor incorrigible are among the most certain beliefs that we have, and more certain than any beliefs that they are based on, e.g. that people need sleep, that Julius Caesar existed, that Australia exists, that Britain is an island. If I am asked how I came to believe that Britain is an island, I will say that my schoolteachers told me so and that I have seen maps of it; but I can think of several things that my schoolteachers told me that turned out to be false, and I have seen maps which include the inscription 'here be dragons'. Moreover I have never sailed round this island. Yet to doubt the insularity of Britain would be lunacy. There is no reason why any subset of my beliefs, defined in terms of their origin, should be the foundation of any other. However, Plantinga concludes that a theist is perfectly in order in claiming that belief in God is one of his or her basic beliefs, and the foundationalist cannot show this to be irrational. I have two things to say about this.

(1) If foundationalism is false, it is not clear that we ought to retain the distinction between basic and founded beliefs at all. Rather let us say that all beliefs should be open to rational scrutiny and criticism. Some will stand up to it better than others, and we may find general reasons why some kinds stand up well; but we should not stipulate that a given belief is basic. To do so would be to remove some beliefs from rational scrutiny, and there would be nothing to stop anyone including the hollowness of the Earth and its habitation by flying-saucer navigators or, worse still, the 'International Jewish Conspiracy', as being basic beliefs, sheltered from criticism.

(2) We need to ask what sort of thing a belief is, and not think that we can solve this question of its rationality or otherwise at a merely formal level, internal to a noetic structure. A belief is a claim about what there is in being. As such, it bears in its own nature the possibility of being tested against the aspect of being that it is about; a belief is inherently vulnerable to testing – to lose that vulnerability is not to gain certainty but to lose all content. There are no a priori constraints on how beliefs might be tested – it depends on the sort of thing the belief is about – but it must be some way relevant to that which it is about. The reference to what it is about and the vulnerability to criticism in the light of soundings made into and information received from what it is about are essential to any belief. Hence the noetic structure must have windows, or better, feelers, if it is to be rational. As we shall see later, the chief error of foundationalism was its underrating of hearsay; if disbelief that Britain is an island is mad, it is

because of the paranoia involved in doubting all the accumulated hearsay to the effect that it is. But the idea of the foundationalists (in their guise as rationalists and empiricists) that reasoning and experiencing have a special role to play as the feelers of the noetic structure was not wrong, even though they theorised reasoning and experiencing wrongly. To this I shall return in chapter 6. My point here is simply that the rejection of foundationalism does not license us to shelter some of our beliefs from the buffets of reasoning and experiencing.

I have discussed four versions of this idea that belief needs no grounds in evidence or argument, and looked at the details of their separate contentions. But at bottom the case against all forms of this view is very simple. We are all familiar – all too familiar – with the phenomenon of wishful thinking. Most people who reject religion regard it as nothing but wishful thinking. It is incumbent upon defenders of religious belief to show that this is not so. But the advocates of belief without cognitive grounds seem to be accepting the charge, and claiming that there is nothing wrong with it. There seems to me to be both a philosophical and a moral error in this position. The philosophical error is that we don't even understand what belief is – how it differs from imagination or hope for instance – unless we recognise that it is a claim to truth, and tacitly a claim to be in a position to argue for or give evidence for that truth. We cannot without deception choose what we believe. Let us take an example from secular studies. Some scholars of ancient societies hold that at the beginning of all human societies there was a period of matriarchy. This was the view of Engels, and several Marxist scholars have followed him. Most scholars deny this, and some hold that matriarchy has never in fact existed. Almost certainly, we have got all the evidence we are ever going to get on both sides of this question, and it is inconclusive. But some people would like one or other of these accounts to be true. For instance, feminists see that if Engels was right, it is shown that male domination is not inevitable, and hence is more likely to be abolishable now.

But even if you would very much like one or other of these alternatives to be true, you can't just sit down and decide to believe it. You may very well be able to come to believe it by wishful thinking, but only on condition that you do not sit down and say 'knowing that there is no way we can find out the truth about this, I am going to believe that Engels was right (or wrong)'. Self-deception only works if one is not fully aware of what one is doing. Nietzsche says somewhere that he noticed a hatred of reason among religious believers and appreciated it, since it was a sign of a bad intellectual conscience. This criticism is entirely justified against this sort of defence (the non-cognitivist) of religious belief. That is the moral point.

# 4 The intelligibility of conversion

One striking feature of the non-cognitive approaches is their incapacity to make the phenomenon of conversion intelligible. It is widely assumed (almost all the students in the course I teach on philosophy of religion assume this) that religious belief is something that you 'either have got or you haven't', and if any explanation is deemed necessary, it is 'upbringing'. Many people who see the matter this way are so out of sympathy with religious belief that they find it unintelligible that anyone could believe unless they had been brought up to do so and had remained uncritical of their received opinions. Conversion, on this account, is unintelligible; it may be admitted that it sometimes happens, but if so it is taken to be an unintelligible happening like a thunderstorm, not an intelligible one like the decision to vote Labour or disinvest in the arms trade or go for a medical check up. But it is curious that some defenders of religion, by their non-cognitive accounts of faith, make conversion unintelligible in the same way. This could only happen in a period in which religion is on the defensive or at least unfashionable, and probably suffering from an uneasy intellectual conscience. The task of defending religious belief is seen as being that of allowing people who already believe to go on doing so without worrying that they might be deceiving themselves. It is a matter of 'ghostly comfort' for intellectual consciences. But if it does convince believers that they need not worry about the arguments against, by the same token it reassures the unbeliever that they don't have to consider the case for faith. And if believers were considering spreading their faith, it must surely tell them not to bother, for there are no grounds for belief and so nothing they can say to persuade the unbeliever. This is particularly blatant on Plantinga's account: the self-doubting Christian may be reassured that it is intellectually respectable to go on believing without grounds, but the Christian who wants to win the world for God will be driven to despair by the thought that he or she can say nothing to unbelieving friends to communicate their faith.

Of the various non-cognitive accounts that I have been discussing, only two seem to have any evangelistic concern: Pascal wants to bribe us into belief by the promise of the hereafter; and Bultmann wants to confront us in preaching with the cross of Christ as the saving work of God, evoking repentance and faith. Indeed, Bultmann's 'demythologising' itself can be seen as having evangelistic goals: the sceptic does not have to be convinced of supernatural events in order to be so confronted. But of course the sceptic does have to be convinced that there is a god and that the cross of Christ was his saving act; otherwise the most that will be evoked is human sympathy for a good man cruelly executed.

However, non-cognitivists may not be worried by my claim that they make conversion unintelligible, since they may admit that it is. Indeed, it is not uncommon for philosophers talking about things far removed from the philosophy of religion, like Kuhnian paradigm shifts (of which more shortly), to say that these are not rationally motivated but are 'like a religious conversion'; it is simply taken for granted that a religious conversion is a change that is not even in intention rational. However, insofar as a religious conversion involves a change of beliefs, it must be that those beliefs were changed either because of good grounds for thinking the new beliefs true, or because of reasons irrelevant to the truth of the beliefs. In the former case the conversion is rational, in the latter irrational. If irrational, it requires an explanation of why beliefs were adopted without good grounds – a psychoanalytical explanation, for instance. But in either case we are dealing with an intelligible change, not a brute fact like the browning of leaves in autumn.

Now it may be said that I am begging the question. For I am claiming that we must treat beliefs as cognitively grounded in order to make conversion intelligible, and then treating conversion as a change of cognitive beliefs, whereas if the non-cognitivists are right, conversion is bound to be a non-cognitive change. I have two things to say in reply: that I challenge the non-cognitivist to give a coherent account of anything deserving the name of a conversion which is non-cognitive; and that a look at actual instances of religious conversions will find them to be cognitive. Not indeed 'merely cognitive'; those still flogging that dead horse the 'head/heart' distinction will say a conversion 'merely in the head' is not enough – it must reach the heart too; I reply that beliefs of the appropriate sort genuinely held will cause emotions and consequently actions unless there is some pathological mechanism preventing them from doing so, and that nothing except those beliefs can cause the appropriate emotions and actions. We can analytically distinguish belief from emotion, but every belief is emotively charged and every emotion is a response to a belief. Although there can be cases of beliefs whose emotions are somehow blocked, or of emotions occurring without the appropriate belief (phobias, for example), a person in whom this process of splitting was so far gone that their beliefs in general formed one system and their emotions in general another, so that you could describe them as having a distinct head and heart, would be severely psychotic.

We have though two rather similar accounts in recent philosophy of phenomena which might be thought to throw light on non-cognitive religious conversion: Kuhn's account of paradigm shifts, and Sartre's account of radical conversion. It is perhaps ironic that after paradigm shifts have been said to be like religious conversion, as if that already gave us a paradigm for non-cognitively motivated change, I am now looking to paradigm shifts to see if perhaps religious conversions could be non-cognitive like them. But perhaps it will turn out that paradigm shifts are not like paradigm shifts either.

In brief, Kuhn argued that, except at times of scientific revolution, any science is governed by a set of concepts and examples constituting a paradigm. Learning the science is learning to use this paradigm, and research takes the form of fitting new data into the paradigm. The paradigm itself is not questioned. Sometimes, though, it becomes more difficult to fit data into the paradigm, and anomalies emerge in the practice of the science under that paradigm. When anomalies accumulate, the science goes into a period of crisis. The crisis is typically resolved when someone – often someone working outside the old paradigm – invents a new one. The concepts of the old paradigm often cannot be directly translated into those of the new one, so rational argument between adherents of the two paradigms does not take place; neither can they agree on a 'crucial experiment' to decide between the two. The new paradigm largely succeeds in replacing the old because adherents of the old paradigm retire and are replaced by adherents of the new one, rather than by the new paradigm converting people from the old one.

Since we are dealing here with bodies of scientific knowledge, it is clear that a paradigm shift, whatever else it may be, is also a change of cognitive beliefs. So it is not a case of non-cognitive change but, at most, non-cognitively motivated cognitive change. However, it cannot entirely be that either, for the motive of change was the accumulation of anomalies in the old theory, and anomalies are cognitive failures – failures in accounting for some aspect of nature which the science in question could be expected to account for. The jump from one paradigm to another, even if not motivated by the cognitive virtues of the new paradigm, is motivated by the cognitive vices of the old one. Furthermore, a new paradigm would hardly be accepted if it had all the same anomalies that the old one did; in some sense, it has got to constitute progress over the old one. And although Kuhn resists the obvious conclusion that this progress consists in closer approximation to the truth, it can hardly be other than cognitive progress, since it is progress in the ability to account for natural processes in a way which avoids anomalies. If it is claimed that the 'incommensurability' of the two paradigms prevents us from saying this, it must be pointed out that the paradigms must at least be commensurable enough for us to say that they belong to the same scientific discipline, that is, are about the same aspect of nature (for example chemistry or botany). Otherwise it will not make sense to say that one has replaced the other.

It is perhaps worth mentioning in passing the unhelpfulness of one metaphor often used to give credibility to a non-cognitivist reading of paradigm shifts: the gestalt switch, like Wittgenstein's celebrated duck-rabbit. Because with gestalt switches we can make sense of the phrase 'seeing things differently' without seeing different things, we assume that this can be made sense of in other contexts too. But gestalt switch pictures are a very special phenomenon; they require an expert draughtsman to do them well – a Dali or an Escher; and they are only possible because of the conventions (not recognised by all cultures) for representing three dimensional objects on a two dimensional surface. Elsewhere in life, there are nothing like gestalt switch pictures, and 'seeing things differently' can only mean seeing different things.

If paradigm shifts form a model for understanding conversion then, it will not be entirely non-cognitive; cognitive defects of the world view converted from will be among the motives of the conversion, and the new belief will at least avoid those defects. For instance, among the many preliminaries to the conversion of St Augustine was his persuasion of the falsehood of astrology by an entirely empirical test: sons were born to a master and his slave simultaneously, and their fortunes in life followed their class not their stars (see Augustine's *Confessions*, book VII, section 6).

Sartre's account of radical conversion may look on the surface less cognitive, and it is also of closer relevance in that it might be thought that religious conversion is actually an instance of such conversion, whereas the paradigm shift is at most a model. Indeed the terms in which he describes radical conversion inevitably suggest religious conversion to the reader: 'self-recovery of being which was previously corrupted' (*Being and Nothingness*, p. 70, n. 9) and 'an ethics of deliverance and salvation' (p. 412, n. 14).

The possibility of radical conversion for Sartre stems from his extreme account of human freedom. On this account, we are not just free to act according to our reasons, motives and values, we are free to choose our reasons, motives and values, and can only have them insofar as we have chosen them. Consequently, our choices can never be justified in terms of these reasons etc., since they constitute them. It is in this sense that our choices are 'absurd'. However, our reasons, motives and values do form a coherent whole at any time, as constituted by a single, complex choice of how to be. Freedom consists not in alternatives within our fundamental choice (there may be such alternatives, but they are trivial ones), but in freedom to change our fundamental choice. Thus the hiker who drops out of the hike when his physically equal companions continue (*Being and Nothingness*, pp. 453ff.) does so because he is a 'sissy' (*douillet*), but being a sissy is an aspect of his fundamental choice. He cannot choose to continue the hike while maintaining his current fundamental choice, but he can make a new fundamental choice and then the motives for dropping out will disappear: his fatigue will no longer be a reason for dropping out, but part of the fun of the hike. This change of fundamental choice cannot happen as a result of voluntary deliberation, which, since it weighs up motives already chosen, is 'always a deception' (p. 450). It is a choice at a much deeper level. And on the surface it looks completely non-cognitive.

If radical conversion is non-cognitive, it will either be incapable of including religious conversion or have to give an account of faith of the sort criticised in the first chapter as faith without belief. Clearly an atheist cannot say 'from now on I will put my trust in God, but without any change in my cognitive beliefs'; perhaps one can imagine an atheist saying 'from now on I will pay far more attention to my feeling of absolute dependence'. Such an atheist, who had perhaps previously only concerned himself with what he could control, opens himself to the passive side of experience, to what is given by nature rather than won from nature, and so on. The conversion of Sartre's hiker that would have enabled him to finish the hike might even have been like this. The most one can concede to Schleiermacher is that such a conversion could be a preliminary to an experience of God. But the *religious* conversion would surely start only with that experience.

But there is more to be said about Sartre's model of radical conversion. For it is not clear that he regards radical conversion as unmotivated: there are no motives outside some fundamental choice, but there may be motives within the old fundamental choice which motivate change of choice; in particular, the realisation that one's fundamental choice is in bad faith will motivate the abandonment of that choice in favour of another. But bad faith is a sort of cognitive error, deceiving oneself, projecting contradictory ends, and so on. It looks as if Sartre's radical conversion is quite closely parallel to Kuhn's paradigm shift, pushed by the discovery of cognitive error, even if not pulled by the discovery of cognitive truth. And as in the case of Kuhn, the new choice will be chosen as escaping, or believed to escape, the error in question. Perhaps another of the preliminaries to Augustine's conversion will illustrate this. He recounts in book VI, section 6, of the *Confessions* that while preparing a lying speech in praise of the Emperor, he passed a drunken beggar who was laughing and joking. 'He was certainly the happier man, not only because he was flushed with cheerfulness while I was eaten away with anxiety, but also because he had earned his wine by wishing good day to passers-by while I was trying to feed my pride by telling lies' (p. 119). This becomes one of the 'pushing' motives for conversion: knowledge that his own way of life was incapable of leading to happiness.

Sartre's notion of conversion then is perhaps not as non-cognitive as it looks. I should say that I am not endorsing either Kuhn's or Sartre's theories here, only saying that they do not give us a non-cognitive account of conversion. But anyway Sartre does not discuss any concrete cases of *religious* conversion; the example of Clovis converting to Catholicism is intended to illustrate a purely tactical, non-radical and not sincerely religious, conversion: Clovis, according to Sartre, becomes a Catholic in order to become king of Gaul. I shall now consider various types of religious conversion with a view to showing that they essentially consist in the effects of new knowledge (or new error). The word 'effects' is crucial here. Conversions are not *just* cognitive; they include changes in emotion and practice, and these are the most striking features of them. But these features are caused by the acceptance as true of new information.

There are certainly conversions which have very little theological aspect, as William James says of the conversion of a drunkard of which he quotes an account (*The Varieties of Religious Experience*, pp. 201ff.). While dead drunk, this man, a Mr S.H. Hadley, 'seemed to feel some great and mighty presence. I did not know then what it was. I did learn afterwards that it was Jesus, the sinner's friend' (p. 202). Hadley vowed not to drink again, got himself locked up for the night to help keep this vow, and went to a mission service next Sunday. He was to become 'an active and useful rescuer of drunkards in New York' (p. 201). To this apparently non-theological (or theological only in retrospect) conversion I shall return. First, it will be useful to consider a class of conversion involving no change in theological beliefs at all, namely conversions occurring in the 'ages of faith', when no one really doubted the propositions of theology as taught by the Church, and conversions had more of the character of calls. The person already believed that God existed, that Christ was his son and that the Church was his authority on Earth, but suddenly came to believe that God had called him or her personally for some special service, or perhaps for the general service that they should have been doing already. Such conversions or calls do not involve change in theological beliefs – not because they do not involve theological beliefs, but because the theological beliefs were already there. But they do involve a new belief, though not a theological one: the belief that one has been personally called by God. In modern times, the way Bob Dylan refers to his conversion looks rather like this:

> Jesus tapped me on the shoulder, said 'Bob, why are you resisting me?' I said 'I'm not resisting you!' He said 'You gonna follow me?' I said 'Well, I've never thought about that before . . .'[1]

In such cases the background of belief may be minimal; just enough for the personal 'tapping on the shoulder' to make sense. Thus this sort of 'call' conversion shades off into the kind where a call comes 'out of the blue', to one who did not previously believe theologically but comes to so believe as a result of an experience of a personal call. Conversions resulting from visions fall into this category. Of course, people do not as a rule have a vision of Jesus or Krishna unless they have heard of Jesus or Krishna, but it is perfectly possible and often actual to have such a vision before believing. St Paul is the classic example, Sadhu Sundar Singh a modern one. Information about Jesus preceded their visions of him, but belief in Jesus did not; both were adherents of other religions. In such cases, the vision is taken as evidence grounding a change in cognitive beliefs – theological as well as personal. Of course, such evidence is fallible, as is all evidence – it could hardly be otherwise since incompatible religions have their respective visions. But that it may be rational to be convinced by it follows, I think, from the argument of the chapter after next.

Hadley's conversion falls somewhere within this spectrum of personal call conversions. The call is experienced first, with presumably some minimum of theological background, but the theological account of the call comes later. Nevertheless, both elements are there in the end: the belief that he had been called, and the belief that it was Jesus who called him.

There is another sort of conversion which also presupposes a background of theological beliefs, but which is importantly different from this. A classic example of this is Martin Luther. He had always accepted the main doctrines of the Church, and had had a 'call' type of conversion when in a thunderstorm he vowed to become a monk, and diligently carried out his vow. However, his notion of God was that of a powerful lawgiver rather than of a merciful saviour, and his emotional commitment to God was consequently lacking. By his own testimony, he secretly hated God. A radical change in his idea of the nature of God, seeing God as he appeared on Calvary rather than on Sinai, changed all this. This is a cognitive change which effected an immediate emotional change, while the background of creedal affirmations remained intact.

Finally, there are conversions which are most obviously cognitive, because there was no background of theistic belief before the conversion, and grounds for such belief were the crucial motivating factor in the conversion. A striking modern case of this is C.S. Lewis. As he recounts it in *Surprised by Joy*, he became philosophically convinced that the objective idealists' philosophical arguments for the existence of the Absolute were good, but that those for the impersonal nature of that

Absolute were bad. So there had to be a personal Absolute, God. This cognitive convincement led to his kneeling in worship, and eventually to a lifelong commitment to Christianity. Although critics have ransacked his biography to look for emotive grounds for his wishing to convert (and of course found them – to whom could such wishes not be plausibly ascribed?), his own account is very different:

> You must picture me alone in that room at Magdalen, night after night, feeling, whenever my mind lifted even for a second from my work, the steady, unrelenting approach of Him whom I so earnestly desired not to meet. That which I greatly feared had at last come upon me. In the Trinity term of 1919 I gave in, and admitted that God was God, and knelt and prayed: perhaps, that night, the most dejected and reluctant convert in all England.
>
> (p. 182)

We have then: (1) conversions presupposing theological belief, and effected by the new belief that the convert was being called personally by God; (2) conversions presupposing theological discourse understood but not yet believed, where a new belief that one is being called forms the grounds for now accepting those beliefs. This can happen against the background of other religions or none. There is a continuum of intermediate positions. In all these cases the belief in the call is accepted on the basis of an experience – an experience which presupposes verbally communicated information, which may or may not have been believed before the experience. (3) Conversions presupposing some theological beliefs but caused by new ones, changing the believer's conception of the nature of God. (4) Conversion resulting from convincement by arguments, of theological propositions not previously believed. All four involve theological propositions, and all four involve accepting new beliefs on the sort of grounds (experience or argument) that other, non-theological beliefs are accepted on.

The third kind is crucial in times of religious revolution, not only the Reformation, but the spread of Christianity in New Testament times too, when the gospel taught a new conception of God as revealed in Jesus to people raised in orthodox Judaism or Hellenistic (poly)theism. There are also elements of it in instances of the other three kinds. The person who receives a call usually thereby comes to see the God who calls them as different from how they saw him before. The convert from one theistic faith to another, like Paul or Sundar Singh, obviously changes their conception of the nature of God. But even when one who had no religious beliefs as these are generally recognised is converted, whether by an experience or an argument, there is often a change in their conception of God: the God they come to believe in is not necessarily of the same nature as the God they had previously rejected. It may be that the reason that they had previously rejected the idea of God is because they had found the conception of God that they had previously had repulsive. There must be something of this in Berdyaev's conversion. In place of the 'sociomorphic' God who is like a tsar or an inquisitor, he sees in Dostoyevsky's tale the Suffering Servant, God on the cross praying for the forgiveness of his torturers. Of course, not all atheists would convert on hearing a new gospel of the nature of God – there are many other reasons for atheism; but some have. Anyway I think this third type of conversion, involving a new conception of God's nature, has a special place in Christianity in that it is central in the New Testament, and fits in with the idea of the work of Christ as being the revealing of God's nature, which is central to John's Gospel.

The fact of scientific revolutions has led many to relativism about science, yet we cannot make sense of *change* in science except as part of a project of acquiring deeper knowledge of nature. It is precisely scientific change that witnesses to the fact that science is not to be explained by its subjects – the scientific community or whatever – but by its object; it changes when it is shown to be inadequate to its object. I focus on conversions for the same reason. If people never changed their religion, a subjective account of religion might do. But since they do, it can only be conceived as a quest for knowledge of something independent of the subject, about which the subject can be mistaken, and which the subject can hope to get to know better, thereby being changed itself. Of course, the fact that religion involves a quest for objective knowledge does not by itself prove that there is anything objective for it to know: it could be a cognitive quest that is doomed to failure by the absence of its object. But failed or not, it is at least a cognitive quest. Not *merely* cognitive of course: faith is an emotion; but like all emotions, it involves belief.

Conversion could of course involve an *irrational* cognitive change, motivated by wishful thinking. But then the fact that it can be criticised as irrational bears witness to the fact that rational cognitive conversion is the norm. But conversion that didn't even purport to have a cognitive motive would be an unintelligible phenomenon which could not, for instance, be incorporated into an account of the person's biographical development. It would be simply a break in that development, like an amnesia. And that is not what real conversions look like.

# 5  About knowledge in general

The traditional arguments for religious belief can be loosely described as either rationalist or empiricist. The ontological argument using no empirical premises and the cosmological arguments using only very simply and universally acknowledged ones are classically rationalist; arguments from design and from religious experience are usually classically empiricist. However, this does not just mean that the former arguments are based on reason and the latter on experience, but that they are based on a particular concept of reason characteristic of rationalism, and a particular concept of experience characteristic of empiricism. Reason and experience must both play essential roles in all forms of knowledge including religious knowledge, but it may well be so, and I believe that it is, that rationalists and empiricists have misdescribed reason and experience. Rationalists typically model reason on geometrical deduction, and empiricists typically model experience on sense perception, conceived as the imprinting of images on a passive and initially blank consciousness. Both are typically foundationalist, holding that there is a special subset of knowledge which is indubitable because of the means by which it is arrived at, and that all knowledge should be founded on this.

Both these theories of knowledge have been severely and I believe cogently criticised in the last century, as not accounting either for our everyday knowledge or for science. No agreed epistemology has replaced them, but in what follows I shall draw out some common implications of two twentieth-century movements of thought which have in their different ways criticised rationalist and empiricist epistemologies. I am referring to the philosophy of science as a separate philosophical discipline, particularly as recently developed by critical realists; and a group of philosophers, most notably Heidegger in Germany, John Macmurray in

Britain and Merleau-Ponty in France, who have focused attention on the knowledge implicit in everyday practice, and who may somewhat loosely be called existential phenomenologists. These two tendencies do not overlap, and are often thought, including by their respective adherents, to be mutually antagonistic. Realist philosophers of science may see existential phenomenologists as irrationalist and anthropocentric, while existential phenomenologists may see scientific realists as privileging science at the expense of other forms of knowledge and as reducing the personal to the subpersonal. While both these accusations may on occasion be correct, these are errors into which these respective philosophies tend to lapse rather than consequences which must follow from their essential premisses. A more fruitful starting point would be to recognise that they are both stressing the peculiarities of the different forms of knowledge with which they are concerned, against the rationalist and empiricist attempts to force the same straitjacket on both. Thus rationalism and empiricism fail to do justice to the need for experiment or its analogues in science, or to the way science discovers depths to nature which untutored observation could never have revealed; yet they also neglect the tacit and practically oriented aspect of most everyday knowledge, and the fact that we experience things for the most part in working on or with them rather than in staring at them. To do justice to both forms of knowledge we must recognise their specificity and difference, and I think there is no doubt that we get a better account of everyday knowledge from the existential phenomenologists and a better account of scientific knowledge from the scientific realists than either the rationalists or the empiricists can give us of either.

Despite the fact that these two modern movements show the distinctness of everyday knowledge and science, they also bring out two shared features of both which have been neglected in foundationalist philosophy. Each has implications which are not always recognised, and which I will draw out at some length. Firstly, both in science and in everyday knowledge we approach the truth by correcting an existing body of partly erroneous 'knowledge', not by preserving the deliverances of an infallible source. In Blake's striking metaphor addressed to the reasoners of Albion 'Establishment of Truth depends on destruction of Falsehood continually, On Circumcision, not on Virginity' (from 'Jerusalem', *Complete Writing*, p. 687). This has sometimes been recognised in the rationalist and empiricist traditions: Spinoza teaches that 'random experience' precedes rational knowledge, which must be won out of it; Bacon contradicts the founding metaphor of empiricist psychology – the blank wax tablet theory of the mind – with the remark:

> On waxen tablets you cannot write anything new until you rub out the old. With the mind it is not so; there you cannot rub out the old till you have written in the new.
>
>          (from 'The Masculine Birth of Time', in B. Farrington (ed.),
>                                  *The Philosophy of Francis Bacon*,  p. 72)

And the logical positivist Otto Neurath has given us the metaphor of knowledge as a ship which has to be repaired while we are still at sea in it. But these are exceptions in a three hundred year tradition of rationalist and empiricist foundationalism.

As against this both Heidegger and Macmurray point out the huge amount of tacit knowledge that is implicit in practice, without which explicit knowledge could never have arisen, and the fact that practical breakdowns reveal the defects in that practical knowledge and motivate the stopping and thinking (Macmurray) or stopping and staring (Heidegger) that give rise to more explicit forms of knowledge. And philosophers of science from Popper to Bhaskar have pointed out that all knowledge is fallible, and that it is not primarily the origin of ideas but their means of testing that makes them scientific.

Secondly, both existential phenomenology and scientific realism are oriented towards practice. When Descartes concentrated on thinking abstracted from practice, and when the empiricists thought of experience as consisting of sense images abstracted from practice, they cut themselves off from the very sorts of reason and experience which give us access to reality, and turned all regions of thought from the world to our ideas about it, and ultimately to our ideas (dropping the 'about it'). But everyday knowledge is above all a feature of practice, largely implicit in everyday practice and corrected in the light of problems encountered in practice; scientific knowledge is entirely the result of a special set of practices, for which people have to be trained and which uncover knowledge which could never have been found without a practice purpose-built for doing so.

On the basis of these two features of knowledge, I shall argue for two positions about knowledge: that the problem of sorting knowledge from error is not a problem of preserving an uncontaminated source of knowledge, but of decontaminating that contaminated source, hearsay; and that knowledge can only be understood in terms of its object, not as the ideas possessed by some subject.

Hearsay is massively predominant in our knowledge. Most of our knowledge is based entirely on hearsay – knowledge of the past, of distant places, of technical subjects on which we are not expert, and most knowledge even of one's own time and locality and of technical subjects on which one is expert. Even that with which we contrast hearsay, namely experience, presupposes and is conditioned by hearsay: we see things in ways derived from language, we largely see those things we have heard about (for instance, we notice a particular kind of bird or tree or flower when we have had them identified to us through language). Even the capacity to check and correct hearsay is one which we have been taught through hearsay.

Of course, hearsay can misinform us, and often does. But the solution cannot be to do without it. People sometimes object to one generation 'indoctrinating' another with 'their' ideas, as if an unindoctrinated generation would find it easier to think for itself; one might as well stop one's children learning one's language, so that they can choose which language to learn, or make up their own, when they grow up. An unindoctrinated (untaught) generation would not be able to think at all. One might as well empty a swimming pool of water, so that people can swim faster without water resistance.

Nevertheless, one must ask how we can check and correct hearsay, since without such a method we have no way of escaping error. And two of the ways available to us are reasoning and experiencing. I use these verbal forms rather than the nouns 'reason' and 'experience' because I think it helps avoid certain misunderstandings. Reasoning is not the application of some special faculty with its own method, like geometric deduction. It is discovering and resolving contradictions among one's beliefs. And experience is not some entity which one could inspect to discover its own nature; it is experiencing something – a transitive verb, used absolutely only as a shorthand. It cannot be understood aside from what is experienced. (While I shall sometimes use the noun 'experience' for convenience or euphony, it must always be read as shorthand for 'experiencing something'.) Experience is conditioned by the hearsay that has preceded it, but not determined by that hearsay: it can refute old beliefs and ground new ones. Experiencing is almost always an aspect of some practice: it is not the sensing of images but working with things and people. Because in doing things we interact with what is outside ourselves and our discourse; reality can surprise us, can hit us in the face and tell us that the received opinions of hearsay were wrong.

In addition to the corrections of reasoning and experiencing, there is one other way that we can be led to question hearsay: suspicion. We may have ideas about what could have led to a particular belief's being part of the received wisdom of hearsay even if it were false, and thereby come to doubt hearsay even without evidence that it is in fact misleading. We say 'they would say that, wouldn't they?', and take care to look again at the evidence before we accept what they say.

These three ways of correcting hearsay each have priority in different ways. Experiencing has priority as the only way that actually brings new information: reasoning may show that one of two beliefs must be false, but not which; and suspicion can show a belief to be unfounded, but not to be false. But reasoning has priority in that any refutation of a belief involves showing its incompatibility with some other belief, so without reasoning experiencing could never refute anything. Finally, suspicion has priority in having the largest scope of the three; we far more often reject a belief because of who holds it than because either reasoning or experiencing compels us to do so. Conversely, we trust hearsay when there is good reason to believe that the authority is in the know, and no reason to believe it is likely to lie or be easily deceived about the matter. Nine-tenths of deciding what to believe is a matter of deciding whom to believe.

Philosophy and scholarship generally before the Enlightenment were much too deferential to authority, although this can be exaggerated – medieval philosophers used reason to decide between or reconcile apparently conflicting authorities. The Enlightenment thinkers were not wrong in pleading for unfettered reason, thinking for oneself and seeing for oneself, judging texts by 'the great book of the world'. But they were wrong to think that one could do this by starting from scratch, cleaning the blackboard and writing on it only what reason or experience could discover unaided by hearsay (which in reality would be nothing). The mistake occurs in the same period in religion as well as in scholarship, in the Quaker aversion to doctrine noted earlier, where it has the same admirable but misguided motives.

The relation of knowledge to what it is about raises the issue of realism versus non-realism. Modern philosophy (meaning here the trajectory of philosophy from Descartes to logical positivism, but living on in 'postmodernism') focuses not on what is experienced but on the experience itself. This has become so much taken for granted that it might seem paradoxical for me to claim that experience can only be understood together with what is experienced, and that only when we have experienced quite a lot of the world and know quite a lot about things that exist independently of us can we turn back to abstract from the experiencing of something the process called 'experience'; and even then, if we ask any questions of experience, it will always answer, like a pointing finger, 'don't look at me, look at what I am about'; this is so whether we are talking about experiences of 'facts' or experiences of 'values'. Modern philosophy, however, makes exactly the opposite assumption: it takes it for granted that we understand what experience is, but that the existence of anything which the experience is about is problematic. The question then arises 'how can we get outside our own experience to compare it with what it is about?', and once this question is asked, it soon comes to be assumed that the answer is that we can't, and it is concluded with Berkeley that ideas are not of anything – though it then becomes entirely unclear what ideas are, since their essence as ideas, surely, is to be of something.

Now this whole retreat from what we experience to the experience itself starts because the sensation of images is taken as the paradigm case of experience. Once it is recognised that we experience things in the main in the course of doing things, we see that the things we encounter in experiencing cannot be left out of our account of experiencing. If we analyse the experience of riding a bicycle or fixing panes of glass in a greenhouse, this is obvious. If we analyse the experience of staring at a coloured shape, it is not: who is to say if the coloured shape is independent of us or not?

> A man that looks on glass,
> On it may stay his eye;
> Or, if he pleaseth, through it pass,
> And then the heaven espy.[1]

Modern philosophy is the philosophy of those who stay the eye on the glass, whether the glass is visual images or language, and regard not only Heaven but Earth as 'well lost'.

I have said that once we ask how we can get outside our own experience and compare it with what it is about, it soon comes to be assumed that we can't. Why is this? The reason is that the person who treats experiences or ideas as entities rather than seeing under cover of these nouns the transitive verbal forms (experiencing something, ideating something) will inevitably treat such comparison as the comparison of one idea with another. I ask my wife where the bottle-opener is, and she says 'in the cutlery drawer'. I look there and find that it is. I may describe my action as comparing a statement with what it is about, but the idealist will say: 'No, you only compared the idea expressed by your wife's statement with the idea you got by looking in the drawer. And in general, all we can compare with ideas is other ideas, not just because (as Berkeley taught) nothing is like an idea but another idea,[2] but because whenever you do the comparing, it is only a new idea that you acquire.' These two accounts can be expressed by the following figure.

my account

the idealist account

Whereas on my account the hearing about and the seeing have the same object (the bottle-opener), and therein lies the comparison, for the idealist I compare two objects neither of which is the bottle-opener, that is, two ideas. But this is because the world has been reduplicated with a world of ideas standing in between us and the world to which we refer. Once this is done, it looks as if we have lost the world beyond the ideas altogether.

Philosophy needs to return 'to the things themselves', in the slogan which Husserl put forward and so dismally failed to accomplish. Existential phenomenology has explored one way of doing this, by starting from an analysis of action rather than pure thought or just staring. As Macmurray puts it:

> How is it possible to test the truth of a thought by a thing? Even if you look at the thing to see if your thought about it is true, you are testing your thought not by the thing but by the visual appearance of the thing, and that itself is an idea, in some sense, because it is 'in your mind'. So runs the argument. And it is a very difficult argument to meet. . . . now, this argument for idealism is only difficult to meet, indeed it only seems reasonable, provided we confine ourselves to a purely theoretical attitude. . . . there is something else besides 'the thing' which we contrast with thought, and that is action . . . the moment we begin to act we find ourselves in contact with things, not with ideas.
>
> (*The Philosophy of Communism*, pp. 23–4)

Scientific Realism has shown another way, with its argument that the whole point of an experiment is that a process set in motion by us shows what tendencies are working when we are not setting them in motion (see Roy Bhaskar's *A Realist Theory of Science*).

I do not want to deny that one can, once one has attained a fairly sophisticated level of knowledge and capacity for abstraction, attend to our experiencings and other ideatings rather than to what they are about, and that it is sometimes useful to do so. We can attend to the glass of the window rather than look through it, and may need to do so if the window is cracked or dirty. But I want to make five claims for the priority of 'the things themselves' to our ideas of them.

(1) Knowledge of our own mental processes is necessarily biographically later than knowledge of the world. We do have to have

arrived at a fairly high level of the capacity for abstraction before we can abstract from the things that we experience or remember and attend to the experiencing or remembering.

(2) The things themselves are ontologically prior in that a thing can exist unideated, but an idea which is not an idea of anything cannot exist.

(3) Things are logically prior to experiences and other ideas in that we cannot define an experience or other idea without referring to things, but we can define things without reference to ideas.

(4) If we accepted the view that since we can only know things by having ideas about them, we can only really know ideas, an infinite regress is generated, for we could only know ideas by having ideas about them, and so on. Related to this is the paradox arising from the attempt to debunk the 'aboutness' of ideas by explaining them. Thus the psychologist may say that the beauty that the lover sees in his beloved is 'in the eye of the beholder', that is, explained by the lover's psychology; but by the same reasoning the neurophysiologist can explain the psychologist's theories as processes in his brain which therefore have no truth value, the economist can explain the neurophysiologist's work as merely a marketable product, and so on. Debunking explanations can be useful where they also show the debunked idea to be false ('explanatory critiques'); but the assumption that any explanation of an idea automatically debunks it as an idea of what it is of is self-undermining.

(5) Ideas borrow their interest for us from what they are about. If they lose their informativeness about their objects, they become redundant. An opaque window is no longer a window.

Now I want in conclusion to make one more point about knowledge in general. I have suggested that science and everyday knowledge cannot be assimilated to each other. While Kant's account of time and space could claim plausibly (if falsely) to be an account both of our common knowledge of time and space and of the way time and space should be understood by science, it is clear that Einstein's account of time and space has no point of contact with our everyday knowledge of them, and that Heidegger's account, which perhaps comes closest to an analysis of our common understanding of them, would be useless to a physicist.

But this is only one fault line in a multiple fragmentation of human knowledge. Science itself exists only as a plurality of sciences, which are not mutually reducible and are divided by real distinctions in their subject-matter. By subject-matter I don't mean the concrete entities which they seek to explain: the Chancellor's budget speech could equally be studied by an economist, a linguist and a physiologist. But even if all three accounts were full and true, there would be little overlap between them.

Everyday knowledge, too, being mainly knowledge implicit in practices, is divided into the knowledge of the gardener, the cook, the motorist, the burglar, the secretary, with little in the way of connecting links. Insofar as different bits of knowledge are linked, it is at isolated crossings rather than along extensive boundaries. The sum of knowledge is like the knowledge of the forest walker of connecting trails through impenetrable woods, not like the knowledge of the geographer who can map the whole forest from a helicopter. It follows from this that bits of knowledge are rarely much help, and should rarely be much hindrance, in pursuing bits of knowledge in other areas. Nothing is more barren than such things as Marxist accounts of language, psychoanalytical accounts of politics, feminist accounts of science or Christian accounts of cosmology – and this is not because of anything wrong with these disciplines, but because cobblers should stick to their lasts.

An awareness of the fragmentation of knowledge should inhibit us from such disciplinary imperialism; it should also warn us against system-building. The old story of the blind men describing the elephant is relevant here: one grasped its tail and said it was like a rope, one felt its trunk and said it was like a hosepipe, one held its leg and said it was like a tree, and so on. The error comes not in the fragments of knowledge but in the assumption by someone who has a fragment that he has the whole story.

One further caution here: it might be said that however partial and fragmented our knowledge is, we can at least know that two inconsistent propositions can't both be true. And that is so. But it very often happens that propositions that were thought to be inconsistent turn out not to be in the light of new knowledge. Not long ago, science and commonsense alike would have told us that curved space or a watch without moving parts was a contradiction in terms. Within any discipline, logical skills – disambiguation, deduction and detection of inconsistency – will help us; but once we stray between our fragmented disciplines, we should not be overconfident even about what seems to result from these.

We have then an account of knowledge which recognises (a) the overwhelming importance of hearsay; (b) that hearsay is fallible and needs to be corrected by logical reasoning, by questioning the reliability of the authorities, and by the test of experience – where experience means primarily learning by living and by practice, rather than sense perception and its analogues; and (c) that knowledge exists as a plurality of knowledges, none of which should be treated as a system which can invalidate the others.

# 6   About religious knowledge

It is the contention of this chapter that religious knowledge is much more like other sorts of knowledge than is commonly thought. Of course there are differences between all areas of knowledge: the abstract sciences are not like the concrete sciences, the sciences in general are not like practical knowhow, knowhow is not like knowing a person, knowing someone else is not like knowing yourself, knowing your own conscious states is not like knowing your unconscious or your character, and so on. Religious knowledge too has its own peculiarities, but no more so than other kinds. Insofar as it is unlike other kinds, it is like them in being unlike. But it is knowledge in the same sense as other kinds of knowledge – it claims to be true about something, and is mistaken if what it is about does not exist or is different from how it is conceived. And its sources are the same as those of other areas of knowledge, namely authority (reliable hearsay), checked and tested by experiences which have themselves been made possible by that hearsay.

Kenny, in his book *What is Faith?*, gives both authority and experience far shorter shrift than other supposed sources of religious knowledge. It will be useful to consider his reasons, for they are very plausible so long as authority and experience are treated separately.

First, authority: aside from the fact that there are many self-styled religious authorities and they all conflict, it looks as though authority could never be the source of religious knowledge, for an authority can only be an authority if its source of information is not authority. A person may be an authority on the way of life in a particular community because they have lived in that community, or on a science because they have themselves performed the experiments which verify that science's theories; someone might be an authority at second hand, because they have diligently studied the words of another authority; but there can be no authority unless it ultimately goes back to a source which is not authority. For to be an authority is to be in a position to know, and unless one knows why a particular person is in a position to know, one will not treat them as an authority. Modern folklorists are familiar with the phenomenon of 'urban legends', those (usually nasty) stories which are passed on as vouched for by someone who knows, but which always turn out when investigated to be hearsay right down to the bottom. Hearsay right down to the bottom is not reliable hearsay. To put it another way, hearsay is second (or third, or Nth) hand knowledge, and is not knowledge at all unless there is first hand knowledge for it to be based on. As Kenny puts it:

> It might be thought that testimony could not be an ultimate source of information: it cannot add to the patrimony of human knowledge, but only circulate existing capital from mind to mind. I do not think this is entirely true: in some areas – the existence of customs and practices, for instance – testimony may be our only source of evidence. But testimony could be given to the existence of God only by reporting experiences of God (and these we have denied to be possible) or arguments to establish God's existence (which will be effective only if natural theology can be successful). The role of testimony in religious belief is not in connection with the existence of God, but in relation to revelation from God.
>
> (*What is Faith?*, p. 46)

In other words, if we already believe in God, we may believe something else is true because we believe God said it; but testimony cannot be ground for belief in God's existence unless it takes us back to some other ground that someone else had for that belief.

This argument seems obvious, and there is indeed something right about it, but it will not do as it stands. The case is much like Spinoza's account of the apparent regress involved in seeking a method to arrive at the truth, for to get a true method one would need a method and so on. He says:

> Matters here stand as they do with corporeal tools, where someone might argue in the same way. For to forge iron a hammer is needed; and to have a hammer, it must be made; for this another hammer, and

other tools are needed; and to have these tools too, other tools will be needed, and so on to infinity; in this way someone might try, in vain, to prove that men have no power of forging iron.

(*Collected Works*, vol. 1, p. 16)

Spinoza points out that from the earliest simple tools we progressed to more elaborate ones, at each stage using tools to make tools. Although this in principle goes back to a first toolmaker who used only what was to hand from nature, it is clear that we do not need to know about primitive humankind with its sharpened flints to understand the technology of Spinoza's time or today. Likewise knowledge by hearsay dates from when our first ancestors received the gift of speech, and we need not know anything about that time in order to understand the role of authority in knowledge today. Certainly in the case of all human individuals, we learn almost everything by hearsay before we experience it, and could not experience in a fully human way without the training given through hearsay. Even a newborn child, long before acquiring speech and thereby hearsay, learns by copying, even within the first few minutes of life. At the other extreme of complexity of knowledge – experimental science – experiments have to be devised in thought, on the basis of the theories that they will verify or falsify, before they can be carried out in practice. Indeed Galileo's thought experiment to show that speed of fall is not determined by weight (in the scientific sense) proved his point better than the practical experiment, which went terribly wrong and only verified the 'law' that experiments never go right first time.

But something must be right about the claim that an authority must show that it is in a position to know, and cannot do this by appealing to authority. What is wrong about it is the idea that the validation of an authority is a matter of seeking origins; what is right about it is that every authority must prove itself at the bar of reason, suspicion and, most crucially for the present argument, experience. In scientific matters, if we believe the scientists it is because we know that they have done the experiments, not because the authorities that taught them how to do experiments had themselves derived knowledge from pure experiment without authority. If we believe the saints about religious knowledge it is because we believe that they have been close to God, not because they achieved that closeness without themselves learning from authorities.

However, Kenny is equally sceptical about experience as a source of religious knowledge. I think part of the problem here is that experience is being assimilated to sense experience as theorised by the empiricists, though as we shall see Kenny's account is superior to a straightforwardly empiricist account such as Ayer's. Ayer thought that experiences are inner sense data, which might make one think that inner religious data are equally respectable. However, Ayer assumes that sense data refer to publicly observable objects, whereas religious data don't. This, however, is assuming what needs to be proved – the religious empiricist would say that God is publicly accessible through religious experiences which anyone can have. At this point Kenny (p. 40) comes to the rescue of the case against religious experience by stating a non-question-begging difference between sense experience and religious experience. Sense experience is experience with a sense organ: we incline our ear to hear what is being said, or turn our head to see what someone is pointing to, or sniff in a sock to see if it is dirty. Religious experience is not given by a sense organ, and therefore one cannot direct someone towards God, or check that what someone else is experiencing is really there by looking in the same direction.

Now I said earlier that religious experience like other kinds of experience does have its special features, and two of these are that God is not located in any one place and that there is no single bodily movement that is involved in directing one's attention to God. But there are publicly communicable rules for getting to know God. Even the mystics, who are often accused of claiming that religious experience is ineffable and then going on talking about it, give practicable instructions. I should say, however, that I am not primarily talking about the experiences of a special class of experiencer – the mystics – when I talk about religious experience. While there is nothing inherently elitist about the idea that different believers should have different gifts – some Bible scholars, some systematic theologians, some mystics, for example – there is a problem in that what Bible scholars and theologians have to say is (or should be) communicable and hence criticisable by others, but what mystics have to say does always seem to point to something incommunicable and therefore uncriticisable, leading to an uncomprehending and therefore possibly misplaced reverence for the mystic. It is for this reason that such incommunicable knowledge (*gnosis*) 'puffs up', as the apostle says; communicable knowledge (*episteme*) need not do so. Furthermore, there are other barriers to following the mystics, which seem to me to be also grounds for suspicion of mysticism. It is perhaps best summed up by one who is sometimes called a mystic himself, though not in the sense of those that I am discussing, namely William Blake:

> The Treasures of Heaven are not Negations of Passion, but Realities of Intellect, from which all the Passions Emanate Uncurbed in their Eternal Glory.
>
> ('A Vision of the Last Judgment', *Complete Writings*, p. 615)

Most of the great mystics show a marked suspicion of intellect and the passions. At least one should give them credit for recognising that these two things – intellect and the passions – stand or fall together, and cannot be set up against one another. But the treasures of mystical experience are generally the denials of both passion and intellect. I do not believe that God gave us these gifts in order to deny them; rather, the intellect should educate the passions by acquiring for them true knowledge of the beings to which they are directed, and the passions thus educated should be affirmed, not denied. I am regretfully aware that this cuts me off from a whole tradition of Catholic and Orthodox spirituality – from the *Philokalia*, from the late medieval German and English mystics, from St John of the Cross and St Teresa of Ávila – but I am enough of a Protestant to think that that is a price that has to be paid. I in no way doubt the genuineness of these people's experience of God, but I do not wish to privilege them over more common types of experience. Furthermore, the religious experience which I treat as evidence is by no means only experience of which God is the direct object, as in mysticism. Such experience has been treated with great rigour and subtlety by William Alston, in his book *Perceiving God*. However, he tends to privilege it at the expense of experience of God through nature or human interrelations, which for me are quite as epistemically significant.

The religious experiences that I am talking about are more what an ordinary Christian may experience coming from taking communion, or in their private devotions; what a Quaker may experience in the silence of the Meeting for Worship; or indeed what many without any religious belief may sometimes experience and interpret in a non-religious way – perhaps also something which we ought to be experiencing all the time if we loved God as we should, and perhaps some saints do.

Now to continue where I left off to discuss mysticism; is there any equivalent to 'turning one's head' in religious experience? Here it is important to recognise that religious experiences are not the private experiences of isolated individuals who must then, afterwards, try to communicate them to people who may have had similar experiences, but without the possibility of comparing them, like Wittgenstein's 'beetle in the box' (each person having a beetle in a box and only ever seeing their own beetle). Religious experiences occur in a tradition, and in the context of a pre-existing public religious language. They occur very often in the context of public religious worship, or private devotions which are also a taught part of religious traditions. These are in a manner of speaking ways of 'turning one's head' to look at God. The apparent barrenness of either authority or experience as sources of religious knowledge comes from treating them separately. The same could be done with science: scientific theories are simply passed on by authority, so they can't have any credibility; but scientific observations are just sense data, which prove nothing about anything except the scientist's own mind. If we had only theory or only observations in science, these criticisms might work. But of course scientific theories generate expectations about the results of experiments, and scientific observations occur as a result of repeatable experiments guided by theories, confirming or disconfirming the expectations generated by those theories. Religion is in some ways like science here; the word comes first: 'faith comes by hearing, and hearing by the spoken word [*rhema*] of God' (Romans 10.17).[1] But having learnt through hearsay what religious actions to take and what religious experience to expect, people find out for themselves whether it works or not. It is like the Samaritan woman's converts (John 4.39–42). Her words aroused their interest in Jesus before they met him, but having met him they relied on their own experience, not hearsay.

However, this embedding of religious experience in religious institutions is the site of another criticism from Kenny:

> We do not argue to the truth of Nazism from fervour of Nuremberg rallies; we condemn that fervour because of what we know of Nazism. So in general: we judge the institution to find out what value to put on the fervour it enshrines and unlocks. We do not regard the fervour as justifying the goals and self-descriptions of the institutions. I conclude that religious experience, in the sense of sentiment

embedded in religious institutions, cannot make the existence of God manifest to the senses.

(p. 39)

There is more than one issue at stake here. The choice of example is presumably meant to show that experience induced by institutions may be not only false but dangerous. And of course Nazism was an evil institution, so it is not surprising that the experiences induced by it – feelings of unconditional patriotism, leader worship, hatred of Jews – were also evil. Here it is worth noting that one teaching of Judaeo-Christian religion is that the way to 'turn one's head' towards God is by practising love and social justice. Thus Isaiah 58.2–11 tells us that God does not 'draw near' to his people when they fast because they oppress the poor; they are urged

> to let the oppressed go free,
> and break every yoke,
> to share your bread with the hungry,
> and shelter the homeless poor

then God will answer when they call, and guide them. This passage is not only a ringing denunciation of social injustice and a programme of emancipation of the oppressed, it is an explanation of the experienced absence of God, and a presciption for opening the way for his revelation. It suggests that the genuinely revelatory nature of the experience induced in a religious institution is conditional on that institution being committed to emancipation, not oppression.

We should not reject all institution-induced experiences just because evil institutions induce evil experiences; the moral here is simply that we should reject evil institutions, 'by their fruits you shall know them'. But there is another issue at stake in the last passage from Kenny, which does not depend on the choice of an evil institution as the example. It may be that the claim is that institution-induced experiences in general – whatever the institution – are just as likely as not to be false. The point is not just that they may possibly be false – this can be taken for granted. No Church teaches that all the religious experiences of its adherents must be true. The point is that there is nothing about an institution that makes it more than a random likelihood that the experiences that it induces will be true. But this is clearly not the case with all institutions. A scientific institution, for example, induces certain experiences in its members by teaching them to read experimental data, and so on. We regard these institution-induced experiences as as authoritative as any. Even a community that does not exist primarily to discover truths, such as a craft community, teaching knowhow in its trade, presumably has some tendency to induce genuine knowledge rather than misconceptions. Some religious communities may be rather like a craft community in this respect. Not all. There are religious propagandists who arouse my suspicion so much that if they told me I was more than three feet tall, I would go straightaway and measure myself to check that I hadn't shrunk. Suspicion here is not a subjective attitude, but an epistemic technique. One does not believe people who habitually lie or contradict themselves or show great credulity, or use manipulative psychological techniques, or have a financial interest in convincing you, or turn their converts into zombies. By their fruits you shall know them.

In arriving at a rational religious belief you have to decide whom to believe, and that decision will not be arbitrary, but will have grounds in the exercise of suspicion, reason and experience. In the end, it will be religious experience that confirms or refutes the word, but, in deciding which word to take seriously, the nature of the authority from whom it comes will play a major role. My claim in quoting the saying 'by their fruits you shall know them' is that, just as in scientific matters the rational thing to do (except where there are grounds for suspicion) is to believe the scientists, in religion the rational thing to do is to believe the saints.

Now it might be said: but scientists are clearly epistemic authorities. Saints are people who seem to us exceptionally good, and in religious terms are exceptionally close to God, but they are not necessarily exceptionally epistemically reliable people. Granted that they are unlikely to lie, they may nevertheless be ignorant, gullible or self-deceived. In assuming that they are not so, at least in the matters that affect their sainthood, I am assuming that virtue always involves knowledge and vice always involves error, that there is a correlation between truth and goodness. I have no space to argue for this cognitive account of ethics here – I have done so at length in my book *Being and Worth*. But certainly great saints close enough to our own time for us to know in some biographical detail – Toyohiko Kagawa, for instance – never strike us as ignorant, gullible or self-deceived.

My conclusion is that the rational grounds for religious belief are the words of the best human beings, tested by reason and experience. I think that these are also the grounds that most thoughtful religious people do actually have for their beliefs. And they are closely parallel to the grounds we have for beliefs about current affairs, science, history, 'the way things are' generally.

To conclude this chapter, I need to reply to the objection that this similarity of religious to other belief can't hold, because religious language is so unlike other language. The strongest version of the claim is that religious language is 'nonsense'. This is a special sense of 'nonsense', in which nonsense can't be true or false, because it has no meaning. Very often we call things nonsense without this implication. If someone tells me that Margaret Thatcher did great things for Britain, or that the Earth is filled with orange marmalade, I would say that that was nonsense, but I would not fail to understand it. I would be saying that it was false, but so numbingly false as to be a ridiculous thing to say. However, when philosophers talk about nonsense they mean what cannot be understood, so that there is nothing in it to be either true or false. Ayer, for instance, claims that his position on religion is not strictly atheism, since atheism states that there is no god, while he holds that the word 'God' is meaningless, and hence that all sentences in which it is used are nonsense. When a philosopher, particularly a Wittgensteinian, tells you that he or she does not understand what you mean, he or she is almost certainly not expressing puzzlement or asking for clarification, but saying that you are talking nonsense in this sense.

There are two very odd things about this claim. Firstly, consider the fact that, for example, Thomas Aquinas wrote several million words in Latin, most of which would count as nonsense in Ayer's terms, but which have been translated well or badly into many other languages, interpreted and counter-interpreted, argued for and against, and so on. It is just not clear how any of these things could be done with words that had no meaning or truth value. It is clearly not nonsense in the sense of non-lexical sounds. But if that is so, secondly, the question arises how Ayer knows that it is nonsense. To do so, he had to read and understand it. But if it can be understood, it is not nonsense.

The truth is (and this is clear enough in the case of Ayer) that the nonsense claim is actually an epistemological claim disguised as a claim about language. Sentences are said to be nonsense if they cannot be verified or falsified. But then two things can be said: that language is not tied to epistemology in this way – we can very easily make up sentences which we can all understand but which could never be verified or falsified; and that the argument required to resolve the issue is the epistemological argument to which most of this book is devoted, not a separate argument belonging to the philosophy of language. In other words, it is being claimed that what we can't know about we can't speak about and, if this were so, a proof that we can know about God would make the argument that we can't speak about him a non-starter.

However, there are philosophers who use the word 'nonsense' in this special sense, yet are not logical positivists like Ayer and do not share his epistemology. Indeed, for many such philosophers, philosophy is precisely about differentiating sense from nonsense, not about differentiating truth from falsehood (as it was for pre-Cartesian philosophy) or certainty from doubtfulness (as it was for post-Cartesian philosophy). For these philosophers, nonsense is the obverse of what they call 'conceptual truths'. It is my contention that, just as there is no such thing as nonsense in the special sense that I have been discussing, so also there are no conceptual truths. Conceptual truths are presumably supposed to be things true by virtue of the meaning of some concept. But this can only really apply to trivialities like 'all bachelors are unmarried'. Genuine non-trivial truths are all contingent – truths about the way things are, not the way they must be. Conceptual truths, insofar as they are billed as non-trivial necessary truths, are in reality tricks for making ordinary empirical truths (or indeed falsehoods) look like logically necessary truths, so that what contradicts them is said to be 'nonsense'. The way it works (and the error involved in it) is like this: we have the concepts that we do because things are the way they are (or appear to be the way they appear to be). If things were radically different, we would have different concepts, and when things turn out to be different from what they seemed, we change our concepts. But the believers in conceptual truths claim that things could not be otherwise, because how they are follows from their concepts. For instance, an eminent philosopher, when asked to give an example of a conceptual truth, gave 'a child marooned on a desert island would die'. Presumably the idea was: 'it is part of the concept of a child that it is dependent for its life on adults; anything that could live without adult support could not properly be called a child.' But we can well imagine a species of rational beings whose children could support themselves from birth, as some animals can. Indeed, if stories about children being raised by wolves or bears are true, this paradigm case of a 'conceptual truth' would be an empirical falsehood.

Now there is a certain sort of argument common in analytical philosophy which works by imagining that things are very different from how they are in order to test the meaning of a concept which we have got because of the way things are as they are, and drawing 'conceptual truths' about that concept from this 'experiment in thought'. I will give as an example an argument which was seriously presented to me as an undergraduate student, which was supposed to prove that there can be no afterlife. Of course, whether there is an afterlife or not is a substantive question, and it ought to have been clear that no mere analysis of concepts could supply the answer; any more than the ontological argument, resting as it does on the mere analysis of concepts, could prove the existence of God. But the production of substantive rabbits out of such formal hats is precisely what 'conceptual truths' are for.

The argument goes like this: suppose we assume that whenever someone dies in this world, someone appears in another world with the character and memories of the person who has died. What criterion have we got for saying that they are one and the same person? None, because if we suppose that whenever one person died in this world, two people with their character and memories appeared in the other world, we would have no grounds for saying that one rather than the other of them was the dead person. So it must be part of the concept of personal identity that it is confined to this world, and there can be no identity between a person in this world and a person in another. One might as well say, of course, that we can imagine that whenever anyone had a bath, two exactly similar people came out of the bath, and argue that therefore even now we cannot regard the person who comes out of a bath as the same person who got in it. But what are the errors in this argument? First of all, that it confuses questions about identity with questions about the criteria for identity. It might well be that A was identical with B though we had no criteria by which we could establish this fact. Secondly, if (what I doubt) survival or non-survival of death is part of the concept of personal identity, then the conclusion should be that a believer in life after death has a different concept of personal identity from a disbeliever. In which case the disbeliever's 'conceptual truth' that personhood ends with death will have no force for the believer, and vice versa. Thirdly, if the second scenario were actual – that when one person died in one world, two appeared in another – we would have a different concept of personal identity from either of the two discussed so far. We would say 'when a person dies, they become two people'. Nothing that we would say under those conditions has any bearing on the meaning our concepts have under existing conditions.

The gist of my argument so far is that there are no conceptual truths, and there is no nonsense in the special philosophical sense. But aside from the claim that religious language is nonsense and is ruled out by certain conceptual truths, there are two weaker claims which involve denying that it has truth values (that is, can be true or false). There is the claim that religious language is essentially metaphorical, and that metaphors can't be true or false. And there is the claim that religious language is a special language game, in which such concepts as truth and falsehood, and related ones such as contradiction, don't apply. I shall not stay long on either topic, since the first has been definitively answered by Janet Martin Soskice in her excellent book *Metaphor and Religious Language*, and the second probably collapses into the position defended by Braithwaite, which I have already discussed.

On metaphors I shall confine myself to three brief points: (1) metaphors, even live metaphors in poetry, can be true or false. As C.S. Lewis points out, when Burns compares his beloved to a rose and Wordsworth compares his to a violet, they are saying different things about different women, which someone who knew the women might agree with or contradict.

(2) No abstract discipline – not science, not logic – can work without concepts which were originally metaphorical: wave in physics, structure in sociology and linguistics, market in economics, following in logic, squares in maths.

(3) While it is true, as Thomas Aquinas points out, that human languages are adapted in the first place to the material world and afterwards extended to talk about God (we call him father on analogy with human fathers), if we take the existence of God and the creation of the world and the self-revelation of God to us seriously, this is not just a matter of inadequate and arbitrary human attempts to say something to which no words are appropriate; rather, God created parenthood on analogy with his relation to the Son (and to his rational creatures), and revealed to us the appropriateness of this way of speaking.

When we say *God is good* we mean neither *God causes goodness* nor *God is not bad*, but *What in creatures we call goodness pre-exists in a higher way in God*. Thus God is not good because he causes goodness; rather because he is good, goodness spreads through things. As Augustine says, *because* he is *good*, we *exist*.

(Aquinas, *Selected Philosophical Writings*, pp. 218–19)

Finally, the idea of religion as a different language game: here I shall go to source and look at what Wittgenstein says, rather than discussing his followers. In the end, I think that Braithwaite's account which I have already criticised is the only way of making sense of this position. The leading exponent of the Wittgensteinian point of view is D.Z. Phillips, but if I were to engage with his argument, I should have to spend a great deal of space on his notion of 'grammar' (a notion derived of course from Wittgenstein, and which has nothing to do with grammar in the grammatical sense), showing this concept to be a non-starter. And that would take me too far from the philosophy of religion. Also, I make a general practice in this book of discussing opposing positions through statements of them that already have the status of classics. Only when there is no such statement do I engage with contemporary writers (as in the case of Plantinga). So here I stick with Wittgenstein.

For what Wittgenstein's many examples of brief dialogues in his 'Lectures on Religious Belief' seem to show is that he doesn't think that a religious proposition and the apparently opposite proposition held by a non-religious person contradict each other. Thus:

Suppose I say that the body will rot, and another says 'No. Particles will rejoin in a thousand years, and there will be a Resurrection of you.'
If some said: 'Wittgenstein, do you believe this?' I'd say: 'No.' 'Do you contradict the man?' I'd say: 'No.'
If you say this, the contradiction already lies in this.
Would you say: 'I believe the opposite', or 'there is no reason to suppose such a thing'? I'd say neither.'

(p. 53)

How can we understand what is going on in such a case? It could be (i) that the religious person is making a metaphorical statement and the other person a literal one: in this case it should be easy for them to clear up the misunderstanding, and there is no philosophical problem; (ii) if the believer accepted Braithwaite's account of religious belief, all would be clear; but genuine religious believers don't; (iii) it could be being claimed that there is some more radical incommensurability between the two speakers, so that the one can't understand what the other is saying, and could only understand it if he or she were to get inside the other one's world view. But if the two are so completely baffled at each other's use of language as not to be able to contradict each other, it is incomprehensible how one could enter the other's world view. If the religious language game is meaningful only to the religious, one use of religious language ceases to make any sense at all: evangelism, the use of words to persuade a non-believer to believe. So Wittgenstein's account cannot be a description which could be accepted by a religious believer. It lets religious language be, but rather in the spirit of an anthropologist who wants to preserve the quaint customs of 'primitive' people and does not care for them enough to tell them what he holds to be the truth. As a Christian with a cognitive kind of belief, I find Wittgenstein's account peculiarly insulting compared with the respect shown, for instance, by the honest antagonism of Nietzsche.

In this chapter I have argued that religious beliefs, like other beliefs, are first learnt from the words of reliable others, then tested in experience; the words make possible the experience, but the experience confirms or refutes the words. This is parallel with how other areas of knowledge come about. Hence the argument that religious language is meaningless because it expresses no knowledge is a non-starter.

# 7 The content of Christian revelation

So far the discussion has for the most part abstracted from the question what it is that is actually revealed in revealed religion and believed by believers. It is not for a philosophical text to spell out the details of Christian belief – that is a theological task. But it is necessary to say something about the *sort* of thing that is revealed and believed, beyond the facts that it can be expressed in propositions, communicated by language and believed on similar grounds to other knowledge. There are two traditional answers to this question (to which a third could be added). It could be that what is revealed is the *nature* of God, or the *will* of God. The early fathers and councils of the Church placed all the emphasis on the nature of God, and I think the Orthodox Church tends to follow this. Roman Catholicism, for all its emphasis on moral instruction, has at least enough of the same approach to have avoided including moral beliefs among the dogmas that all Catholics must believe. I don't think that Reformation Protestantism departs from this tradition either, and indeed I have claimed that Luther's conversion was essentially a change of belief about the nature of God. But modern Protestantism (at least since Kant) tends to dismiss teaching about the nature of God as metaphysical speculation, and focus on the will of God.

At one level, it might be argued that the distinction is a false one: when Hosea tells us that God requires mercy not sacrifice (Hosea 6.6) or when Isaiah tells us that he requires social justice not the trampling of the Temple courts (Isaiah 1), they are not only revealing the will of God for us, but his own just and merciful nature; when John tells us that God is love, he is not only telling us about God's nature, but that everyone who loves is born of God (1 John 4.7–8), and hence that mutual love is God's will for us. Furthermore, classical theology (for instance, Thomas Aquinas) teaches that will and nature are not distinct in God.

Nevertheless, there are two reasons why we need to make this distinction and, in my view, come down on the side of the older view not the modern one. Firstly, though nature and will may be one in God, the revelation of God's nature and his will are not one for us, for the revelation of his nature is in the indicative and the revelation of his will is in the imperative. This is not a trivial grammatical distinction. A revelation in the imperative – a set of commands to be obeyed – gives neither grounds for obedience nor the strength for obedience. It is authoritarian in the bad sense, for without knowledge of the nature of God it makes perfectly good sense to ask 'why should we obey God?'. Only a revelation of the nature of God can answer that question. The sort of person who would be willing to obey God whatever his nature would be just as willing to obey Hitler. And such imperatives unfounded in indicative revelation are also ineffective. As Luther puts it: 'The law says: "Do this!", and it never is done. Grace says: "Believe in this one!", and forthwith everything is done' ('Theses for the Heidelberg Disputation', no. 26, Dillenberger, p. 503). For a revelation of the nature of God, unlike an imperative, gives both a reason and a motive for works of love.

Secondly, saying that in God will and nature are one could mean either that God's will is nothing but his nature, or that his nature is nothing but his will. In other words, it could mean that what God wills flows inevitably from his nature as loving, just etc., or it could mean that God has no nature but what he chooses to be. The notion of God as steadfast and unchanging points to the former view, but some might say that if God can't be what he chooses to be, he is not omnipotent. It is necessary to look further into this notion of God's omnipotence as supposedly implying that his nature is dependent on his will.

It is generally recognised that omnipotence does not include the power to break the laws of logic. That is a fact about the laws of logic rather than about omnipotence. Logical impossibility is not like natural impossibility only more so; doing something naturally impossible, like turning water into wine, is doing something, but doing something logically impossible, like making a round square, is not doing anything at all, so the incapacity to do it is no lack of power. As C.S. Lewis puts it, if you make up a piece of nonsense, it doesn't become sense because you say it about God. If 'I can make a round square' is nonsense, so is 'God can make a round square'.

However, there are some things that an omnipotent being can't do, though we can. God can't make a stone so big that he can't lift it. This does not look like a limit to omnipotence since it follows from it (making a stone so big that an omnipotent being can't lift it is like making a round square), though on a certain account of omnipotence it might be claimed that it shows that the concept of omnipotence is incoherent, like the concept of a set that is a member of itself.

The problem gets tougher when we ask whether there are some things that God can't do, not because of his omnipotence, but because of his other properties like omniscience, necessary existence and goodness. And surely there are. God can't forget, or deceive himself, or commit suicide, or do evil. On analogy with the stone example, we can say that making a necessary being cease to exist or a perfect being commit evil is like making an omnipotent being unable to lift a stone, a contradiction in terms. But this does commit us to saying that there are some things which God can't do which, if his nature were different from what it is, he could do (and beings with other natures can and do do); in other words, that God's will is limited by his nature, though not by anything outside his nature. His freedom is Spinozan freedom (freedom to act according to his nature), not Sartrean freedom (freedom to choose any nature). That this does not commit us to Spinoza's pantheism can be illustrated by the answer to another supposed limit on God's omnipotence. Can God create a valid £5 note? Spinoza would say yes he can and does, because the Banks of England and Scotland, which alone can do this, are modes of God. A theist in the Judaeo-Christian tradition would say no he can't, because he is distinct from his creatures. But this too is part of God's nature.

Is this account of God's omnipotence compatible with biblical teaching on the subject? I think it is. The word translated 'almighty' in the Old Testament (Shaddai) does not have that meaning. It may come from the Hebrew word for breast (shad), and signify 'provider'. The Greek word 'pantocrator' means 'ruler of all', and is a metaphor from earthly rulers, who are far from determining everything that happens in their realms. The saying, in connection with the tricky business of getting camels through needles' eyes and rich men into the Kingdom of God, that all things are possible with God is quite naturally read as meaning that God can do anything he chooses without the implication that he can choose anything. Other passages suggest that there may be constraints even on God doing what he chooses, though these constraints must surely in the last analysis be the constraints of his own nature – of which more later.

Does the Bible in fact purport to reveal God's nature, or only his will? In the Old Testament, which might be thought to be more will-oriented, there is a running battle between the worship of Yahweh and that of other gods. Yahweh *is not* Baal or Moloch. But Yahweh is the only god that exists, so why should we not say that 'Baal' and 'Moloch' can only refer to Yahweh, so that the god worshipped by the Hebrews under the name Yahweh and the god worshipped by the Canaanites under the names Baal and Moloch were one and the same? The reason is that the nature of Yahweh is not the same as the nature attributed to Baal and Moloch. This is reflected in the etymology of the names: 'Yahweh' alludes to being ('I am that I am'), while 'Baal' ('master') and 'Moloch' ('king') refer to human relations of domination. Hence Hosea can say:

When that day comes – it is Yahweh who speaks –
she [Israel] will call me, 'My husband',
no longer will she call me, 'My Baal' [master].

(Hosea 2.16)

But above all their different natures are shown in their different tastes in worship – worship by justice and mercy, or worship by sacrificing children. The prophets were at the job of showing us the nature of God against false gods – and also false conceptions of God himself. For they are almost as scathing about the worship of Yahweh by Temple services and sacrifices as they are about admittedly pagan worship, demanding instead the ending of oppression and the relief of poverty, and honest and loving relations between people. And these are not arbitrary fiats – they flow from the nature of God presented by the prophets as that of a father who cannot stop loving his disobedient son and a husband who cannot stop loving his adulterous wife.

However, if the nature of God is revealed in the Bible, it is not in the Bible considered as a sum total of propositions, but above all in the unique revelation of God in Christ, to which the Bible is witness. This immediately organises the Bible, and gives certain parts priority over others, as Luther saw in his Preface to the New Testament. Within the Old Testament the pre-exilic prophets and Deutero-Isaiah come to the fore, not only as prefiguring the revelation of God in Christ most fully, but as the texts in terms of which Jesus himself understood his mission. The Gospels are naturally the core of the New Testament. But it is in John's Gospel that the nature of revelation is raised explicitly. For the Synoptic Gospels, Jesus is first and foremost the bringer of the Kingdom of God, and for Paul he is the reconciler of God and humankind by his death, but John sees him most saliently as the one in whom God's nature is revealed:

> John 1.18: 'No one has ever seen God; the only Son, who is in the bosom of the Father, he has made him known.'
> John 14.8–10: 'Philip said to him "Lord, show us the Father, and we shall be satisfied." Jesus said to him, "Have I been with you so long, and yet you do not know me, Philip? He who has seen me has seen the Father; how can you say, "Show us the Father"? Do you not believe that I am in the Father and the Father in me? The words that I say to you I do not speak by my own authority; but the Father who dwells in me does his works." '
> 1 John 1.1–2: 'That which was from the beginning, which we have heard, which we have seen with our eyes, which we have looked upon and touched with our hands, concerning the word of life – the life was made manifest, and we saw it, and testify to it, and proclaim to you the eternal life which was with the Father and was made manifest to us.'
> 1 John 4.9: 'In this the love of God was made manifest among us, that God sent his only Son into the world, so that we might live through him.'

We have here the strongest impression of those who knew Jesus personally feeling that they knew God the Father by knowing him,[1] and can commend the same means of knowing God to those who come after and hear the gospel story. The answer to the question 'what is God's nature?' is given by answering the question 'what was Jesus's nature on Earth?' We are learning about the nature of the Father as well as the Son when we read that Jesus was one among the poor, who had nowhere to lay his head; that he was a friend to outcasts, even befriending a rich but socially outcast cheat and bringing him to repentance, yet gave to Temple profiteers only a sound beating and the loss of a day's profits; that he met freely with women, treated them as friends and welcomed them as disciples, at a time and place where it was said:

> If a man gives his daughter a knowledge of the Law it is as though he taught her lechery.
>
> > (R. Eliezer, quoted by Jeremias,
> > *Jerusalem in the Time of Jesus*, p. 373)

and in which:

> Rules of propriety forbade a man to be alone with a woman, to look at a married woman, or even to give her a greeting. It was disgraceful for a scholar to speak with a woman in the street. A woman who conversed with everyone in the street could, like the woman who worked at her spinning in the street, be divorced without the payment prescribed in the marriage settlement.
>
>    It was considered preferable for a woman, and especially an unmarried girl, in general not to go out at all.
>
> > (*ibid.*, p. 360);

that he was harsh only to the self-righteous and to the rich who would not relinquish their wealth; that he prayed for the forgiveness of those who tortured him to death; that he was no snob or prig or killjoy, but could be plausibly described as a glutton and drunkard and keeper of bad company. The miracle stories too tell us something about what God values: life, health, sanity, relief of hunger, a good revel at a wedding; nowhere does he tell sufferers that they should resign themselves to their sickness or bereavement as God's will; nor does he turn wine into water as so many later disciples would like to do. Here we have a combination of life-affirming values with commitment to the oppressed and afflicted – a combination which, as Nietzsche rightly pointed out, is rare enough. However, the point is not just that Jesus endorses these values by his behaviour, but that he shows thereby what God the Father is like. And indeed, this revelation of God in Christ is summed up right at the beginning of John's Gospel in the title he gives to Christ: 'the word'. As St Ignatius of Antioch (possibly a disciple of John's) put it, 'there is One God Who manifested Himself through Jesus Christ His Son, Who is His Word, coming forth from silence' ('Epistle to the Magnesians', *The Epistles of St Ignatius*, p. 58). God is no longer silent: his self-revealing word is Jesus. Of course it is the words of Jesus as well as his other actions that reveal God, and in some ways even pre-eminently so; yet the words, and particularly those on the subject of his own person, would carry little conviction without the character revealed in his actions. And his actions include his death as well as his life – again, in some ways pre-eminently so. Yet I think that John, unlike some later theologians, sees the Passion as a consequence of the incarnation rather than its main purpose.

Alongside this conception of Jesus as revealer of God's nature in his own person, there is another feature of John's teaching about revelation. This is the recurrent metaphor of light:

> The true light that enlightens every man was coming into the world.
>
> (John 1.9)

Jesus is seen as the light both in the sense of the one who gives light to humankind and in the sense of the one who throws light on humankind, showing us up, for both senses are reinforced elsewhere in the Gospel:

> If any one walks in the day, he does not stumble, because he sees the light of this world. But if any one walks in the night, he stumbles, because the light is not in him.
>
> (11.9–10)

> Jesus said to them, 'The light is with you for a little longer. Walk while you have the light, lest the darkness overtake you; he who walks in the darkness does not know where he goes.'
>
> (12.35)

But on the other hand:

> And this is the judgement, that light has come into the world, and men loved darkness rather than light, because their deeds were evil. For everyone who does evil hates the light, and does not come to the light, lest his deeds should be exposed. But he who does what is true comes to the light, that it may be clearly seen that his deeds have been wrought in God.
>
> (3.19–21)

Jesus, by revealing God's nature, is also revealing the world as God's fallen creation. In several passages this is linked both to judgement and to testimony, about both of which the teaching of this Gospel seems paradoxical at first: God is said to have delivered the judgement of the world over to the Son (5.22, 27). Yet Jesus says 'I judge no one' (8.15). The judgement it seems is passed neither by Father nor Son, but by the light itself (3.19), or by the word:

> 'I have come as light into the world, that whoever believes in me may not remain in darkness. If any one hears my sayings and does not keep them, I do not judge him; for I did not come to judge the world but to save the world. He who rejects me and does not receive my sayings has a judge; the word that I have spoken will be his judge on the last day.'
>
> (12.46–8)

One is reminded of the truth commissions set up in some newly liberated countries, notably South Africa, which aim to bring the crimes of power to light, not in order to impose a separate punishment on them but to judge them by the exposure itself. Jesus brings the light: the light both gives us something to walk by, and judges our wrongs. What is the light? Surely the revelation of the nature of God in Christ.

The question of Jesus's testimony as to himself is also raised in this connection, in one of the most paradoxical passages in this Gospel:

> Again Jesus spoke to them, saying, 'I am the light of the world; he who follows me will not walk in darkness, but will have the light of life.' The Pharisees then said to him, 'You are bearing witness to yourself; your testimony is not true.' Jesus answered, 'Even if I do bear witness to myself, my testimony is true, for I know whence I have come and whither I am going. You judge according to the flesh, I judge no one. Yet even if I do judge, my judgement is true, for it is not I alone that judge, but I and he who sent me. In your law it is written that the testimony of two men is true; I bear witness to myself, and the Father who sent me bears witness to me.' They said to him therefore, 'Where is your Father?' Jesus answered, 'You know neither me nor my Father; if you knew me, you would know my Father also.'
>
> (8.12–19)

Here Jesus admits bearing witness to himself, yet claims corroboration from the Father; but the Father's evidence is known only through his own ministry. The argument depends on the last sentence: if they knew Jesus, they would know the Father through him; his witness is self-authenticating because it is transparent to the witness of the Father. It is this transparency that the whole Johannine corpus sets forth. It is interesting that, in older versions of the Bible, the story of the woman taken in adultery appears immediately before this passage. Most modern scholars regard it as out of place there, but if so then the editor who placed it there was no fool. It illustrates the nature of judgement by light, acquitting one whose guilt is apparent, convicting those whose guilt is hidden.

On the surface it would seem that these questions of how the world is judged and how Jesus's authority is vindicated seem distinct, though the symbol of light as that which (as it appears to us, not as it is explained by physicists) shows both itself and what it shines upon can stand for both. But the interlinking of these themes in John suggest that for him who (if we take the ultimate source of this Gospel to be the apostle John) knew Jesus personally, that knowledge at one stroke reveals the nature of the Father, the Sonship of Jesus, the fallenness of the world and the way that we should live in it. And it is by communicating this knowledge that Jesus saves the world: 'this is eternal life, that they know thee the only true God, and Jesus Christ whom thou hast sent' (17.3).

I mentioned a third alternative to the ideas that revelation was of God's nature or of God's will. This is the idea that it is of God's acts. If God's acts mean the life, death and resurrection of Christ, then there is much to be said for this view, which I suspect both Bultmann and most evangelicals would endorse. However, on the view defended here, the acts are themselves primarily revelations of God's nature, the word of God to humankind. This might be questioned from the standpoint of St Anselm's theory of the atonement, but I think it is consistent with everything in John's Gospel. I would not wish to deny what the other Gospels teach about Jesus as bringer of the Kingdom or what Paul teaches about the atonement as reconciliation, but (a) these are also aspects or manifestations of the nature of God, and (b) they in turn have to be revealed to us through the word and become part of our knowledge of God. So I do not think my claim that what is revealed is knowledge of the nature of God, and that this itself is (as John tells us) 'eternal life', contradicts the Christology of the Synoptic Gospels or Paul; it merely situates it.

In this chapter I have discussed what sort of knowledge religious knowledge is – what it is about. I have defended the coherence of one account, which I believe to be the Christian account: that it is knowledge of the nature of God, as revealed in the historical person Jesus Christ. Of course this view is unique to Christianity, and not held by all Christians.

# 8 The knowledge of God as creator

I have been defending the rationality of belief in revealed religion. Arguments to the existence of God from the natural world I have rejected as philosophically inconclusive and theologically objectionable. Now it might be objected: even if arguments for God's existence from the nature of creation do not work, once we have accepted God's existence on other grounds, we can learn something about God from creation. Unless we deny (as Marcion did) that God is the creator and sustainer of all things, we can learn from the existence of roses, rabbits and rainbows that God created roses, rabbits and rainbows, and so presumably something about the nature of God – namely that he loves roses, rabbits and rainbows. As Maimonides and Spinoza put it, the more we know about particular things, the more we know about God.

There is some truth in this, but we need to take care with such arguments. For the theological objection to arguments from nature to God still holds: the ruler (or rulers) of this world according to the New Testament are powers of evil, not God; 'the whole world lies in the power of the Evil One' (1 John 5.19). If we arrive at beliefs about the nature of God from studying the nature of nature, we may well argue from 'nature red in tooth and claw' to a god red in tooth and claw. Perhaps the most sinister thing about Hick's 'vale of soul-making' theodicy is that in order to show that the god of this world is good, he had to redefine good and evil,[1] so that the evil in this world is seen as good in that it 'builds character' in a Spartan or public school sense. Nature worship quite naturally leads to copying the cruelty of nature – from the Canaanites' religion's sacrifice of children to the Social Darwinism of Spencer or Hitler.

And yet the power and beauty of nature have a spontaneous religious appeal, which any mind not dulled by commercialism must feel. It is felt alike by Jews and Christians, polytheists and pantheists, Wicca and dialectical materialists. One can find it in atheist poets like Shelley and MacDiarmid and Marcionite poets like Blake, as well as theistic and pantheistic poets. It might be claimed that pantheism and polytheism are the most natural, spontaneous expressions of this feeling. Polytheism in particular, with its recognition of the irreducible multiplicity of natural forces, and its feeling for particular places, seasons or processes as special manifestations of these forces, seems to be *the* natural form of religion for human beings. Pantheism is a more intellectual religion, into which polytheism easily develops once it is subjected to rational reflection, as in Stoicism and Hinduism (which is not to say that it is more defensible than polytheism). The emotive attractiveness of pantheism is borrowed from polytheism, I think. When we read in Spinoza of 'God or Nature', we respond because we have experienced the sacred in hills and forests and waterfalls. But of course Spinoza's 'Nature' also includes not only the ugly and destructive parts of what we call 'nature' – decaying carcasses, birds of prey which peck out the eyes of living animals or pluck smaller birds alive before eating them, fatal viruses – but also human products such as napalm, or cities with sewage running down the streets where people live. For all my admiration of Spinoza (I see him as 'the philosopher', as the medievals saw Aristotle), polytheism is much more defensible, intellectually and morally, than pantheism. If we did not have the revelation of God through the prophets and in Christ, we ought all to be polytheists.

But whether or not polytheism is a more spontaneous expression of the religious impact of nature than others, the appeal to nature as an expression of the divine is common to Judaism and Christianity as well (Psalm 104, Jesus's reference to the lillies of the field in Matthew 6.28–9, Paul's claim in Romans 1 that God is manifest to gentiles through creation).

I think the following points sum up the truth about this feeling for the holy in nature.

(1) This feeling is part of the 'religious a priori', affecting all spiritually healthy people whether atheist, theist, polytheist or pantheist, and forming one motive for and element in all religious beliefs.

(2) We must assume that in itself it is unspecific between various religious beliefs, since it is compatible with all these beliefs. It does not *prove* any of them, or indeed anything: it is a feeling not an argument.

(3) In the absence of revealed religion, it has historically tended to lead in the first instance to polytheism. There is some reason to regard this as the most 'natural' expression of uninstructed religious feeling. It captures the particularity of the natural phenomena that evoke the sense of the holy, and the plurality and diversity of forces generating natural phenomena. Since these forces are indifferent and often destructive to human ends, it is also quite natural that some form of bloody sacrifice, including human sacrifice, should be part of most polytheistic religions, and the more so the more that they are nature-religions. I am not just talking about Baal and Kali. The argument 'nature does it so it must be right' lives on: in Social Darwinism letting the weakest die in its liberal forms or killing them in its fascist ones; in conclusions sometimes drawn from the Gaia hypothesis; and in some recent versions of socio-biology.

(4) It nevertheless forms an indispensable element in revealed theistic religion. It is clear that the Hebrew prophets and Jesus and Paul all take it for granted that God the Father is the creator and sustainer of all things. This is supplemented by John's teaching that Christ as the *Logos* is the one through whom all things were created (John 1.3), and Paul's that in Christ all things hold together (Colossians 1.17). And when Christianity found its first great philosopher in St Augustine, faith in God the creator is made the foundation of ethics, though in quite a different way from the *copying* of nature of which the Canaanites and Social Darwinists have been guilty. For as Mill pointed out, nature commits against us all those crimes for which, when done by one human to another, we reserve the harshest punishments.

In Augustine, God is good, and all being is good because it is God's creation. However, there are degrees of being and therefore a ranking of goods: God is the highest good, people are higher goods than irrational animals, sentient animals than insentient plants, and all life forms than inorganic matter. Even inorganic matter, though, is good in its degree. We ought to love all things in proportion to their goodness – not their moral goodness, but their degree of being: God first, then people, then animals and so on. Evil consists in preferring lesser goods to greater, for example preferring the creature to the creator or material wealth to living creatures, and so on. To this ethic (which I subscribe to), and its differences from the pagan ethics of copying nature, I shall return.

First, though, I need to answer the main question of this chapter: how can we reconcile what we know about God from his revelation in Jesus Christ with what we know about God from creation?

I have been defending a concept of revelation as cognitive: what is revealed is knowledge about the nature of God. But for the revelation, we would not have that knowledge:

> No one has ever seen God; it is the only Son, who is nearest to the Father's heart, who has made him known.
>
> (John 1.18)
>
> To have seen me [Jesus] is to have seen the Father.
>
> (14.9)

This knowledge displaces all other conceptions of deity which we might have, including those derived from 'creation theology'. It shows God as one who loves and sacrifices himself for those he loves; who forgives and requires mutual forgiveness among people; who comes to save life not to destroy it; who is drawn to the poor, the despised and the broken, and is intolerant only of the self-righteous; who will not break a bruised reed or quench a smoking flax; who is born in a stable not a palace, and rides a donkey not a war-horse; who does not dispute that the kingdoms of the world are in Satan's power to give, but will not do what is necessary (join Satan's party) in order to win them. This knowledge of God not only displaces all 'natural religion', it also answers that hostility to the god of natural religion – god as the ruler of this world – which has led so many to atheism. 'God was in Christ reconciling the world unto himself' – not, as St Anselm thought, reconciling himself to the world, but among other things telling the militant atheist 'I am on your side – the god of this world really is the enemy'. The world, as Luther put it, is a tavern whose landlord is a robber – but God is not that landlord.

But if God the creator has the nature that is shown in the life, teaching and Passion of Jesus, why does the world that he created commit such serious crimes against us? Is there not a huge discrepancy between the nature of God as revealed in these two ways: God with pierced hands and a crown of thorns, or a god red in tooth and claw? The God revealed in Jesus is a god who *cares* for nature, and who therefore does not will it to be red in tooth and claw – yet in some measure (not entirely) it is. Jesus's saying about the sparrows is surely meant to indicate that God cares about them – yet they still fall to the ground. The Calvinistic New International Version of the Bible (and some other modern versions) tell us that the sparrows don't fall without the *will* of the Father – as if God were to say 'Ha ha, little sparrow, I've got you now! Out you go to your death – plop!' – like some callous, nest-robbing lout. But this is a falsification of the text – the Greek does not contain the word 'will'. Rather it is implied that God knows about the sparrows and cares for them, but for some reason cannot stop them falling to their deaths. We should not shrink from saying this; there are many things that a being possessing 'all possible perfections', including omnipotence, could not do. Many of them are things that people can do, as we have seen. Aside from things that are logically impossible for God, there are things that he can't do because they are against his own nature. Spinoza is surely right that God's infinitude can only mean that he is not limited by anything outside himself. I have argued that not only human beings but even God can only have a Spinozan freedom, not a Sartrean one – freedom, that is, to act in accordance with one's own nature, including one's knowledge of the nature of other beings, not freedom to act unconstrained by any nature. I suspect that one of the things that God can't do without going against his own nature is to violate the nature of any of his creatures, even when doing so would be the only way of preventing wrong being done.

There are passages in the Bible suggesting that the laws which currently govern nature are not altogether the laws that God wills to govern nature. For instance, Isaiah promises that in the Messianic Age animals, including humans, will be mutually harmless (Isaiah 11.6–9). Probably when Mark tells us that Jesus in the wilderness was with the wild beasts, he is referring to the first fruits of this Messianic Age (Mark 1.13). Paul writes of creation groaning to be freed from its slavery to decay (Romans 8.19–23). According to this last passage, not just humankind but nature too is fallen. Of course, we cannot theorise this fallenness, as Jews and Christians before the scientific age did, as a fall brought about by events within human history – the sin of a historical Adam – which had a chain reaction through nature. However, those who did so may have captured certain aspects of the truth. Thus Augustine (*City of God*, book XIV, chapter 15) suggests that 'the retribution for disobedience is simply disobedience itself'; that is to say, human disobedience to God resulted in the 'disobedience' of the parts of the human body to their owners. Extending this a bit, we have an image of the fall as the *falling apart* of a universe that had previously held together in harmony, with the beings that were further from God in nature obeying those nearer to God in nature, and all creatures obeying God; with our bodies offering no resistance to our intentions, and humankind, as Augustine also says, ruling 'irrational creatures' – not indeed as 'Lords of beings' but as 'shepherds of Being', to use Heidegger's distinction. With the fall, things that had previously been united fall apart into a war of all against all, species against species, person against person, bodily organ against bodily organ. Each entity becomes at once *destructive* because it is set against other entities in a struggle for existence, and *destructible* since its parts no longer cohere but tend to fall apart and hence become vulnerable to the aggression of other individuals.

Now if this account remains what it was for Augustine, a historical account of what happened at some point in time, within (if early in) human history, it is of course scientifically untenable. Matter had the same fragile structure that it does now millions of years ago; dinosaurs tore each other to bits millions of years before humans existed, and our hominid ancestors clubbed their prey – and doubtless each other – to death with scant regard for 'humane' considerations long before we achieved the status of *Homo sapiens*.

But it is possible to see creation, throughout the whole of its history known to us, as bearing not only the marks of its divine origin (as many theologians have taught) but also the marks of its fallenness. It is important to avoid dualism here. The idea is not to divide up creatures into 'goodies' and 'baddies', since God made the Tyger as well as the Lamb. We must accept that since God is the creator and sustainer of all things, 'being as being is good' (Augustine), and evil is a privation or disintegration of being. But we can discern the privation (destructiveness and destructibility) as well as the being in all creatures.

One approach to this is through another one of the concepts that the medievals called 'transcendentals'. Crudely stated, transcendentals are concepts which apply to everything. The central one is *being* and all other transcendentals are convertible with being; that is to say, they mean something different from being, but apply to everything that being applies to. Thus, since being as being is good, the terms 'being' and 'good' are convertible – in modern terminology, they have different senses but the same referents. There are five transcendentals according to medieval philosophy: being, good, truth, beauty and unity (oneness). The one I want to discuss here is *unity*.

To say that unity is a transcendental is to say that everything that exists has unity. A tree must be one tree. Of course, there may be many wood cells in the tree, and many trees in the forest. But there cannot be a wood cell unless there is in it some inner coherence by virtue of which it is *one* wood cell; there cannot be a tree unless all the wood cells in it cohere in such a way that it is one tree; and there cannot be a forest unless the trees cohere in some such way as to make it one forest. So the idea that unity is a transcendental does not commit us to what Leibniz meant when he said that there is no entity without unity; he meant to deny that there could be composite entities, which commits us to a single layer of indivisible entities. My claim on the contrary is that there are many levels of composite unities, but that the unity of a composite is a real structured coherence, a matter of the inner relatedness of its parts.

There is nothing mysterious about the view that all beings have oneness. You can transplant all the trees of the forest to different parts of the world; you have still got trees, because each tree retains its oneness, but you have no longer got a forest, because it does not; you can separate all the cells in the tree; you have still got cells because each retains its oneness, but you haven't got a tree, because it does not. So to say that God is the sustainer of all things (in being) is the same thing as to say that in him all things cohere (in oneness). To talk about evil as a corruption of being (that is, a corrosion, a rusting or rotting away) is the same as to see it as a dispersion of composite beings into their component parts. The mark of God in creation is the gatheredness of creatures, that is, the co-operation of many individuals together in some larger entity: of cells in a bodily organ, organs in a body, people in a community, and so on. The mark of fallenness is their dispersedness into competing individuals, threatening the existence of the larger individuality. In the case of any individual, this dispersedness has two aspects; that the individual is set against other individuals to the detriment of larger wholes; and that its parts are set against each other to its own detriment. In two words, fallenness (dispersedness) consists in the destructiveness and destructibility of all individuals. Contrary to these marks of fallenness, one can focus on the (inner) coherence, and cohesiveness (with other individuals in some larger whole) of entities. In these features, one sees the marks of their createdness by God.

This chapter has been more theological and more specific to Christianity, rather than concerned with issues which arise in all theistic religions, than the earlier chapters. Yet it is essentially concerned with the philosophical task of exploring apparent contradictions. I have tried to answer the question: if God is revealed only in Jesus Christ, yet is revealed as creator, what place can there be for a theology of creation?; it seems both necessary and impossible. I conclude that a theology of creation is part of Christianity, but it must learn to discern (on the basis of the revelation of God in Christ) what in nature and history reflects the nature of the creator, and what is the result of fallenness and alienation from the creator. It must at all costs avoid the blasphemy of treating everything that happens as the will of God.

# Notes

### Introduction

1  See his *Scientific Realism and Human Emancipation,* chapter 2, section 5. See also my *Critical Realism*, chapter 6.
2  See my discussions of Spinoza's ethics and moral psychology in my *Being and Worth*.
3  Some version of the Kantian argument that 'existence is not a predicate' has to refute the ontological argument; and I have yet to see a version of the cosmological argument that did not rest on the doubtful assumption that there can be no infinite series of causes.

### 2  Faith without belief II

1  In passing it may be noted that this last quote is sandwiched between two statements which can hardly both be true: 'The needs of practical life require that a body of believed propositions should be purged of inconsistency.' And 'Indeed a story may provide better support for a long-range policy of action if it contains inconsistencies.'

### 3  Non-cognitive grounds for belief

1  See his book *What is Faith?*, discussed in chapter 6.

### 4  The intelligibility of conversion

1  From the notes to the CD *The Bootleg Series*, on the song 'Ye shall be changed'.

### 5  About knowledge in general

1  From George Herbert's poem/hymn 'Teach me, my God and King', in *Hymns Ancient and Modern* (Revised), no. 337.
2  As for this view that an idea can only be like another idea, it is just a plausible but clanging falsehood. It is like refusing to sign the back of a passport photo to vouch that it is 'a true likeness', saying that a photo can be like nothing but

another photo. Like in some respects, yes; but we don't know what a photo is unless we know that it is a more or less true likeness – and so with ideas.

## 6 About religious knowledge

1 Margaret Archer has convinced me that there are some human experiences that owe nothing to language, and some religious experiences might fall into this class. I continue to suspect that any such experiences would be interpreted in a polytheistic way, and therefore lead one into false beliefs, without input from the word.

## 7 The content of Christian revelation

1 I follow John A.T. Robinson (see his *Redating the New Testament* and *The Priority of John*) in holding that the Johannine writings go back to an eyewitness account, probably that of the apostle John. I am aware that this is a minority opinion among scholars, most of whom date the Fourth Gospel from the last decade of the first century. But even if they are right, the local knowledge present in the Gospel suggests an earlier text behind the edited text, and one written by someone who knew Palestine and hence could well have been an eyewitness.

## 8 The knowledge of God as creator

1 See his *Evil and the God of Love*.

# Bibliography

Alston, W. (1991) *Perceiving God*, Ithaca and London: Cornell University Press.

Aquinas, T. (1993) *Selected Philosophical Writings*, Oxford: OUP.

St Augustine (1961) *Confessions*, Harmondsworth: Penguin.

—— (1972) *City of God*, Harmondsworth: Penguin.

Bhaskar, R. (1978) *A Realist Theory of Science*, Hemel Hempstead: Harvester.

—— (1986) *Scientific Realism and Human Emancipation*, London: Verso.

Blake, W. (1966) *Complete Writings*, London: OUP.

Bultmann, R. (1960) *Jesus Christ and Mythology*, London: SCM.

—— (1964) *Existence and Faith*, London: Fontana.

—— (1964) *Kerygma and Myth*, London: SPCK.

—— (1965) *Theology of the New Testament*, London: SCM.

—— (1961) *Faith*, London: Adam and Charles Black.

—— (1966) *Faith and Understanding*, London: SCM.

Burns, R. (1963) *Poems and Songs*, London: Dent.

Collier, A. (1994) *Critical Realism*, London: Verso.

—— (1999) *Being and Worth*, London: Routledge.

Dillenberger, J. (1961) *Martin Luther*, Garden City, New York: Doubleday Anchor.

Farrington, B. (ed.) (1966) *The Philosophy of Francis Bacon*, Chicago: University of Chicago Press.

Haldane, R.B. (1903–4) *The Pathway to Reality*, London: John Murray.

Hick, J. (1968) *Evil and the God of Love*, London: Fontana.

*Hymns Ancient and Modern* (Revised) (1981) Norwich: Canterbury Press.

St Ignatius (1919) *Epistles*, London: SPCK.

James, W. (1912) *Essays in Popular Philosophy*, New York: Longman.

—— (1982) *The Varieties of Religious Experience*, Harmondsworth: Penguin.

Jeremias, J. (1969) *Jerusalem in the Time of Jesus*, London: SCM.

*The Jewish New Testament* (1999) Baltimore, USA: Jewish New Testament Publications.

Kant, I. (1873) *Critique of Practical Reason*, trans. Abbott, London: Longman.

—— (1964) *Critique of Pure Reason*, London and New York: Macmillan.

Kenny, A. (1992) *What is Faith?*, Oxford: OUP.

Lewis, C.S. (1977) *Surprised by Joy*, London: Fount.

Macmurray, J. (1933) *The Philosophy of Communism*, London: Faber and Faber.

Mitchell, B. (ed.) (1971) *The Philosophy of Religion*, Oxford: OUP.

Pascal, B. (1960) *Pensées*, London: Dent.

Plantinga, A. (1979) 'Is Belief in God Rational?', in C.F. Delaney (ed.), *Rationality and Religious Belief*, Notre Dame.

Robinson, J. ( 1978) *Redating the New Testament*, London: SCM.

—— (1985) *The Priority of John*, London: SCM.

Sartre, J.-P. (1957) *Being and Nothingness*, London: Methuen.

Schleiermacher, F. (1996) *On Religion: Speeches to its Cultured Despisers*, Cambridge: CUP.

Soskice, J.M. (1985) *Metaphor and Religious Language*, Oxford: OUP.

Spinoza, B. (1985) *Collected Works*, Princeton: Princeton University Press.

Tillich, P. (1953 (vol. 1), 1957 (vol. 2), 1964 (vol. 3)) *Systematic Theology*, Welwyn: James Nisbet.

Wittgenstein, L. (1966) *Lectures and Conversations on Aesthetics, Psychology and Religious Belief*, Oxford: Blackwell.

# Name index

Alston, William 81
Anselm, St 99, 104
Aquinas, Thomas 4, 11, 85, 88, 89, 91
Archer, Margaret 110
Aristotle 102
Augustine, Aurelius 27, 56, 57, 58, 103,
    105, 106
Ayer, Alfred 80, 85, 86

Bacon, Francis 67
Berdyaev, Nicholas 12, 30, 31, 62
Berkeley, George 70, 71
Bhaskar, Roy 1, 67, 72
Blake, William 34, 66, 81, 102
Braithwaite, R.B. 28–34, 44, 88, 89, 90
Bultmann, Rudolf 39, 41–8, 54
Burns, Robert 24, 88

Darwin, Charles 10,
Democritus xi,
Descartes, René xi, 67, 70
Dostoyevsky, Fyodor 30, 31, 62
Dylan, Bob 59, 109

Einstein, Albert 73
Engels, Frederick 50

Fell, Margaret 19
Fox, George 19

Galileo 10, 79
Godwin, William 5
Grellet, Etienne 20

Haldane, R.B. 21
Hare, R.M. 28
Heidegger, Martin 41, 47, 65, 67, 73, 106
Herbert, George 109
Hick, John 101, 110
Hobbes, Thomas 5

Hume, David 1, 5
Husserl, Edmund 72

Ignatius of Antioch, St 96

James, William 38–41, 59
Jeremias, Joachim 3, 96
John of the Cross, St 81

Kagawa, Toyohiko 84
Kant, Immanuel 5, 13, 18, 23–8, 34, 35,
    36, 40, 41, 73, 91, 109
Kenny, Anthony 48, 77, 80, 82, 83, 109
Kierkegaard, Soren 33
Kuhn, Thomas 54, 55, 56, 58

Leibniz, Gottfried 107
Lewis, C.S. xii, 60, 61, 88, 92
Luther, Martin xii, 2, 21, 60, 91, 92, 94,
    104

MacDiarmid, Hugh 102
Macmurray, John 65, 67, 72
Maimonides, Moses 101
Marcion 101, 102
Marx, Karl 34
Merleau-Ponty, Maurice 66

Neurath, Otto 67
Nietzsche, Friedrich 50, 90, 96

Ockham, William of 5, 33
Origen 10

Pascal, Blaise 35–8, 54
Paul, St 4, 22, 42, 60, 62, 99, 100
Phillips, D.Z. 89
Plantinga, Alvin 48–51, 53, 89
Popper, Karl 67

# Subject index